FOCUS ON
SPEAKING

Anne Burns   Helen Joyce

National Centre for English Language Teaching and Research

Focus on speaking

MACQUARIE
UNIVERSITY ~ SYDNEY

© Macquarie University 1997
Reprinted 1999, 2002

Published and distributed by
National Centre for English Language Teaching and Research (NCELTR)
Macquarie University
Sydney 2109

ISBN 1 86408 297 6
ISSN 1327 7316
1. English language – Study and teaching – Foreign speakers. 2. English language
– Spoken language. I. Joyce, Helen. II. National Centre for English Language
Teaching and Research (Australia). III. Title. (Series: Focus on … (North Ryde,
N.S.W.); 2).

The National Centre for English Language Teaching and Research is a
Commonwealth Government-funded Key Centre for Teaching and Research
established at Macquarie University in 1988. The National Centre forms part of
the Linguistics Department within the School of English, Linguistics and Media
at Macquarie University.

The Publisher would like to thank the following for permission to reproduce
copyright material:
Addison Wesley Longman, Harlow for an extract on page 28 from *Language as
discourse: Perspectives for language teaching* (1994) by M McCarthy and R Carter.
Prentice Hall, Upper Saddle River for extracts on page 47 from *English for Adult
Competency* (1981) by Keltner, Howard and Lee.
Australian Government Publishing Service for an extract on page 49 from *Talk
back: Elementary* (1980), for Figure 7.1 on page 105 from *Australian Second
Language Proficiency Ratings* (1981) by D Ingram and E Wylie and for extract 6
on page 49 from *Situational English for newcomers to Australia: Part 1,
Teacher's Book* (1976).
National Food Industry Council for Table 4.1 on page 60 from *Effective
communication in the restructured workplace: 1. Team work – a training
program* (1995) by H Joyce, C Nesbitt, H Scheeres, D Slade and N Solomon.
NSW AMES for Figure 7.3 on page 110 from *Certificate II in Spoken and
Written English*, (1995) and for extract 4 on page 49 from *Toubled Waters
1&2, Teacher's Guide* (1994) by S Cornish.

Disclaimer
While every care has been taken to trace and acknowledge copyright, the
publishers apologise for any accidental infringement of copyright where
the source of material is unable to be traced.

Cover design: Michael Gormly, Superkern Desktop
Design: Jane Parish Graphic Design
Desktop publishing: Nicole Williams, NCELTR Publications
Printed by Robert Burton Printers Pty Ltd

CONTENTS

CHAPTER

	To the reader	iv
ONE	Understanding speaking	1
TWO	Producing and negotiating spoken language	17
THREE	Theoretical perspectives	39
FOUR	The speaking needs and goals of language students	53
FIVE	Planning for speaking in the language program	69
SIX	Speaking activities in the classroom	81
SEVEN	Assessing speaking	101
EIGHT	Common questions about speaking	115

TO THE READER

Who is this book for?

This handbook has been written as an introductory text on teaching speaking to adults. It has particular relevance to teachers of English as a Second Language (ESL) or English as a Foreign Language (EFL), but it will also provide helpful information and advice for teachers of adult literacy, teacher educators and vocational trainers.

If you are a student teacher you may be looking for an overview of theoretical issues and practical ideas for teaching speaking in a language program.

If you are an experienced language teacher you may be looking for guidance on how to better integrate speaking into your teaching program, or you may be looking for answers to some specific questions – for example what methodologies might be most appropriate for a particular profile of learner. On the other hand, you may simply want to refresh your thinking on the teaching of speaking and to use this book as a resource to stimulate new ideas.

This book has been written in response to requests from teachers, student teachers and teacher educators. It is a resource which aims to help you to:
- understand more about the process of speaking
- understand more about how spoken language differs from written language
- identify particular student needs in relation to speaking
- design courses which integrate the teaching of speaking
- choose spoken texts and design activities
- assess speaking.

An overview of the book

The first three chapters in this book explore general issues in relation to spoken language and teaching speaking. The remaining chapters focus more specifically on course planning and teaching.

Chapter 1 explores the nature of spoken language and examines why and how we learn to speak our mother tongue. It focuses on the social role which spoken language fulfils and some of the skills involved in speaking. It also examines how spoken language differs from written language. Chapter 2 focuses on a number of key issues to do with the production of spoken language and the negotiation of meaning between speakers. In Chapter 3 we provide a brief overview of the key theories of speaking which have informed teaching over recent years. We also consider the theoretical ideas that are currently helping to shape the pedagogy of speaking. Shifts in theory are never accompanied by an immediate wholesale change in teaching practice and you are invited to consider what theoretical notions are reflected in your own teaching practice.

Chapters 4 to 6 focus on practical ideas and offer guidance for teaching speaking. Chapter 4 provides a detailed discussion of learner needs. A number of student and class profiles are presented with notes on the implications for teaching speaking. You are invited to consider your students' needs in relation to various criteria.

In Chapter 5 we focus on planning for a program and provide guidance in sequencing content and establishing goals and objectives. Samples of programs based on topics and texts are presented. Special attention is given to integrating speaking with other language skills.

Chapter 6 provides some pointers on the selection of texts for teaching speaking. This chapter offers a wide variety of sample activities including preparatory activities and activities which focus on speaking strategies and on language awareness. The activities are presented only as illustrations and examples. You can adapt them to your own situation and use them to generate many other ideas.

Chapter 7 focuses on different types of assessment of speaking including placement, diagnostic, formative and achievement assessment. Examples of different methods of assessment are provided.

Chapter 8 features ten commonly asked questions about teaching speaking. We use these questions as a basis for discussion of issues in speaking pedagogy rather than as a way of offering unequivocal advice.

How to use the book

The chapters in this handbook are designed to be read in the order in which they are presented. However, it may be that you want to focus on a specific chapter because it relates to a segment of your training course or because it focuses on an issue of particular interest to you. For this purpose each chapter has been designed to be as self contained as possible, and we provide cross-references to other chapters in relation to some key points.

The wide left-hand margin can be used for making notes as you read and some chapters have a blank page at the end for further notes.

Prereading questions

Each chapter, apart from the last, includes some prereading questions. Spend some time thinking about the questions and, if possible, write some notes in response. Having attended to these

questions, you will find that your reading of the chapter will be more focused and you will recall more of what you read.

Tasks within chapters

From time to time within a chapter you will be invited to undertake a task. You may be asked simply to think about your own views on something before you read on, or to read a particular text and respond in some way to it or to reflect on issues it raises in relation to your students. Although the temptation may be to skip over the task and read on, where possible take the time to do the task. It may help to clarify ideas for you and we hope it will make your reading more enjoyable.

Chapter reviews

All chapters, except for Chapter 8, conclude with a brief summary of the main topics and ideas presented. When you complete a chapter, read through the review and consider what you have learned from reading that chapter.

References

References are provided at the end of each chapter and after the questions in Chapter 8. As you are reading the book you may come across a reference that is especially relevant to your work. Make a note of it immediately or highlight it in some way so that you can readily retrieve it when you have time to access a library or catalogue. As this resource is intended as an introductory text we recommend that you follow suggestions for further reading in the areas that are of special interest to you.

ONE

UNDERSTANDING SPEAKING

Think about four different social situations in which you have spoken today:

- Who were you speaking to?
- Were you speaking to people who were familiar or unfamiliar to you?
- Why were you talking to them?
- What were you talking about?

Think about the task of speaking in these four different situations:

- Did any difficulties occur? Why was this?
- What did you do to make the speaking situation more successful? Did you:
  - ask the speaker to repeat information?
  - ask for further details?
  - indicate to the other person that you were following what they said?

What is speaking?

Almost all of us learn to speak and in fact speaking is so much a part of daily life that we tend to take it for granted. However, learning to speak involves developing a number of complex skills and different types of knowledge about how and when to communicate.

It is useful when thinking about speaking to consider how we develop speaking in our mother tongue. If you have had any contact with very young babies you will know that although they cannot speak, there still appears to be some kind of communication taking place. This involves interacting with those around them through different types of cries, different sounds, various lip movements and facial expressions such as smiles and frowns. Family members often react to a young baby's smiles or gestures as if they were turns in talk.

To go beyond this very early stage young babies must develop a number of verbal skills as preparation for speaking. They must listen to and try to imitate the sounds of the language made by the people around them. This is the point when learning to pronounce the sounds of the mother tongue begins. Usually at around six months babies begin to utter sounds which have particular meanings attached to them. These are not recognisable words and often the only people who can understand their meaning are the caregivers. This stage, before actual language use has developed, has been called the proto-linguistic stage (Halliday 1975).

Vocabulary or content words are the first recognisable elements of spoken language to develop. At about 12–14 months, young children are usually moving into this stage where, much to the delight of the parents, they begin to utter single words such as 'Mumma' or 'Dadda'. This is the beginning of verbal skills development and it will continue throughout their lives. The single word stage develops rapidly and in their second year of life children learn to name a whole range of things in their familiar and immediate environment. At this stage pronunciation is still developing and sometimes people who do not know the child may have difficulty understanding what the child is saying.

Children soon progress to the multiple word stage where they rapidly learn to put words together to create more complex meanings (eg 'Daddy go work' or 'John buy ice-cream'). Grammatical words – such as pronouns, prepositions, verb auxiliaries, conjunctions and so on – tend to develop later.

Making meaning

Young children learn very early that speaking is about making meaning. The sounds and the grammatical structures of our mother tongue are our linguistic tools for exchanging meanings with each other. As children begin to speak they also learn that

CITY OF WOLVERHAMPTON COLLEGE

speaking enables them to participate in social situations and interact with other people. As speakers they can:
- ask for things that they want
- get other people to respond to their requests
- express who they are as individuals
- socialise with those around them
- explore their world and find out how things work
- verbalise things that go on in their imagination
- exchange information with other people.

Spoken language in context

One of the most important aspects of speaking is that it always occurs within a context. When we speak we are both using language to carry out various social functions and choosing forms of language which relate in a relevant way to the cultural and social context. Although we may not think about it consciously, we attune our language and the meanings we wish to make to the context and to our purposes for speaking within that context. To see how the language and the context work together we can look at some short examples of people using spoken language.

TASK 1.1

Read the following examples of spoken language and answer the questions below (S = Speaker).

1 What contexts do you think these examples come from?
2 What features of the language allow you to identify the context?
3 What is the topic of the interaction?
4 What kind of relationships do the speakers have in these contexts?
5 What aspects of the language allow you to identify these relationships?

Example 1
S1: With Dr Maitland? Right … that's four o'clock on Wednesday then, Mrs Aboud.
S2: OK, that's fine.

Example 2
SI: How many passengers?
S2: Two
S1: Going to?
S2: International Airport
S1: Address?

Example 3

S1: So, after that I went straight to the toy shop to get some …

S2: Milk and … one sugar or two?

S1: Two, please …

S2: Yeah … did they have any?

Examining Example 2, we see that it is part of a telephone exchange between an employee and a customer. We can identify the context from terms such as *passengers, international airport,* and *address,* and recognise the overall topic of booking a taxi. The two speakers are not known to each other and they focus only on the immediate purpose of the interaction. They are formal and distant with each other. The language is made up of a series of short questions and answers. This is because it is a commercial situation where the taxi company needs only to know a few very specific details in order to supply the service. Also the company must allow for incoming calls from other customers and time is very important. In different speaking situations, this abrupt and direct questioning sequence would appear rude.

Reasons for speaking

A common sense explanation of what happens when people speak to each other is that they are 'making conversation'. However, in everyday life we speak for many different kinds of reasons as the examples in Task 1.1 show. Some of these reasons are to do with our desire to relate to each other as people, while others have to do with exchanging information or seeking a practical outcome. In this book we use the term interaction rather than conversation to apply to situations where speaking is taking place.

We can explore the idea of different reasons for speaking a little further. Think about the speaking situations you identified in the prereading task. You may have been involved in situations such as the following:

- telling children to get ready for school
- chatting with a neighbour about the nice weather
- telephoning the garage to book a car in for a service
- discussing holiday plans with workmates
- telephoning your mother to ask her to pick up the dry cleaning
- gossiping with friends about a common acquaintance
- discussing your son's progress with his teacher
- answering a sales enquiry at work
- making an appointment at the post office to order a new passport
- discussing promotional prospects with a supervisor at work.

In each case you would have been exchanging meanings for a particular reason. Sometimes this would be to exchange pleasantries and to oil the social wheels, as in the conversation with the neighbour or the discussion about holidays with workmates. These kinds of exchanges can be called *interactional* (Brown and Yule 1983; McCarthy 1991). At other times the speaking would have had a practical purpose, such as making the appointment for a new passport, the sales enquiry or the discussion about promotion. These kinds of interactions are often called *transactional* (Brown and Yule 1983; McCarthy 1991).

In each context you would have been constantly taking into account your relationship with the person(s) you were speaking to. This is a particularly important aspect of speaking; for example, if you telephoned your mother to ask her to pick up your dry cleaning, you would probably exchange pleasantries or personal news as well, in order to maintain your familiar social relationship. Many speaking situations can be a mixture of interactional and transactional purposes.

TASK 1.2

Look again at the list you wrote for the prereading task. Decide which speaking situations were mainly transactional, which were mainly interactional and which were a mixture of both?

How is speaking related to listening?

In interactions, we take on the role of both speaker and listener alternately. Although the skills of speaking and listening are often considered and taught as separate macroskills in language teaching, in everyday life we need to be speakers and listeners at the same time. These skills are dependent on each other rather than independent.

As speakers we must choose language which takes into account our listener's current knowledge or point of view on the topic. We must also be sensitive to the listener's feedback and pick up signals that indicate whether our message is clear or is being misunderstood, and whether it is interesting to the listener. We may have to repeat, clarify or extend our meanings according to how we assess this feedback.

As listeners we need to be able to interpret the input we are receiving and to provide feedback that indicates we are responding. If we have not understood the message we need to be able to suggest that we have a comprehension problem by asking the speaker to repeat, to clarify or to expand on what has been said. In spoken interactions the speaker and listener build up the meanings together. If we consider how speaking and listening work together in everyday situations we can see that

spoken interactions involve a joint activity where the speaker and listener are actively matching various kinds of knowledge, such as knowledge of:

- the way language works (eg the sounds, grammatical structures and meanings)
- the current situation (eg where it takes place, who is involved and what has already been discussed)
- the way interactions generally proceed in such situations (ie the accepted or usual ways of jointly developing conversations)
- the world in general (ie cultural or social information which speakers bring to bear on interpreting what is being said).

Read the following interaction and answer the questions below ([= overlapping speech).

1 How skilful are the two people as speakers?
2 How skilful are the two people as listeners?
3 Is this exchange a successful one in your opinion? Why, or why not?

A: And then Jeremy arrived …

B: Who's Jeremy? [Does he work with you too?

A: [He didn't even mention the fact that he was half an hour late, which was incredibly embarrassing at this point..

B: Who's Jeremy? I can't see why being late …

A: Yeah … just so embarrassing. Typical of him, isn't it?

You may have identified a number of communication problems in this short interaction:

- A does not seem to take into account the state of B's knowledge of the people or the situation being discussed.
- When B questions A about Jeremy, A ignores the request for clarification and does not stop to provide the kind of feedback which would assist B's comprehension.
- A also continues with the story, the main point of which relies on a shared knowledge about Jeremy's lateness.
- When B repeats the question about Jeremy's identity and asks about his lateness, A again fails to provide clarification and repeats the point instead.
- A expects B to have enough shared knowledge to understand the information being given and to agree with the evaluation of Jeremy's behaviour.

As the focus of this book is on the teaching of speaking, we will not be exploring the issue of listening in great detail. However, the links between speaking and listening are taken up again briefly in Chapter 8 and suggestions are made for integrating these two skills in teaching.

The nature of spoken language

When we look at actual samples of speaking that have been transcribed, we are often surprised that they are very different from the way we think people talk. We also begin to realise just how different speech is from writing when we examine spoken language data such as the following – an excerpt from a casual conversation involving Paula:

> I know when Sydney had the Bicentennial celebrations in 1988, I don't know... for some reason I never went to any of the fireworks, never, you know... and they had all these fireworks for this and fireworks for that... and then last year I went in and saw the fireworks for real for the first time and I was so amazed how different it is to what I'd seen on TV... I mean, I'd have just sat and watched anything from the TV thinking, oh its much better on the TV, we can see it better... but it just doesn't capture the atmosphere.

One of the first things we notice is that when speech is written down it appears far more disorganised and chaotic than written language yet in real spoken interactions speakers are readily able to understand and respond to each other. This suggests that speech, far from being disorganised, has its own systematic patterns and structures – they are just somewhat different from those in written language.

In the firework example, the interaction takes place face to face amongst a group of neighbours who are enjoying a cup of coffee together. Paula can assume that she and her listeners already share information about certain events like the public firework displays that are common in the centre of Sydney during celebrations. She does not need to talk about these events explicitly, but can assume that when she says 'the fireworks' and 'I went in' her listeners know what she means, because they share the same cultural and situational knowledge.

In order to tell the story, Paula adds detail, shaping the story as she continues to talk. She does this by stringing together new pieces of information, often using linking words such as 'and' and 'but' as she keeps the talk going. Speakers aim to sound fluent and so stock or formulaic phrases such as 'I don't know', 'for some reason', 'you know' and 'I mean' are often used. Speakers also draw on these kinds of routine set expressions, which are not typical in written language, to help them put forward their opinions. Speakers also use informal forms of language that are generally only found in speech, such as 'for real' or 'TV'.

A written version of the same story would be much shorter, but at the same time more explicit in setting the context for the reader. There would be far less repetition when referring to the

main topics (fireworks). Writing also tends to stick more to consistent grammatical structures. A written version would be unlikely to involve the changes of pronouns Paula employs when she moves from *I* to *they* to *we* or to use the pronoun *it* to refer to the fireworks. A written version which Paula may put in a letter might look something like this:

> I went to the New Year Fireworks on Sydney Harbour this year. It was the first time I've ever gone. I didn't even go during the Bicentennial celebrations in 1988. I usually watch them on television but it was very different seeing the real thing. Television can't really capture the atmosphere of the crowds and the excitement.

Read the following example and answer the questions below.

1 What context is the speaker referring to?
2 What shared knowledge does the speaker take for granted? Find examples of this in the language used.
3 What linking words does the speaker use to keep the talk going?
4 What expressions does she use for fluency?
5 What expressions does she use to express her opinions?
6 Are there any expressions which are more typically used in speech than writing?

You weren't there last Saturday, even though it was windy...the weather had actually dropped when we were on the courts, you know, it wasn't nearly as bad as I thought it would be...though I was tempted not to go, mind you, because it wasn't half windy...and Wai said no we're going.

Spoken language compared with written language

The scripted dialogues which appear in many language teaching resource books are typically based on grammars of English derived from written language. However, speaking in real-life interactions is not a matter of producing a spoken version of written language. Speech is a way of achieving a range of communicative purposes which are different from those achieved through writing. Thus, it is not the case that speech is inferior to writing, but rather that speakers use the resources of language differently from writers.

In language teaching it is useful to be able to pinpoint some of these differences between speech and writing; the first and perhaps the most obvious difference being that speech and writing are typically used in different kinds of situations. When we speak we are usually interacting directly with others (eg telephoning to make an enquiry about goods and services or chatting casually to friends in our lunch break). The language we produce is spontaneous and relatively unplanned and as a consequence we tend to use more informal or everyday language that does not always conform to standard grammatical conventions of written language. On the other hand, when we write, we are generally alone and not in direct contact with the people to whom we are writing. We have more time to plan what language we will use and to reflect on the topic of our written text. Writers also often feel under an obligation to achieve accuracy and precision, because written language is more permanent than spoken language.

Make two lists side by side, one listing typical situations where spoken language is used and one where written language would be the most common mode of communication.

It is not only the situations in which spoken and written language are used that are different. There are differences also in the language patterns which are selected by speakers and writers. One major contrast lies in the extent to which the language interacts with the actual context itself. A piece of writing has to be able to exist away from the physical context in which it was produced. It needs to be self explanatory and the reader needs to be able to access the meanings from the text itself. In speaking situations, however, speakers can use the surrounding context to make meanings; for example, they can refer to things in the context as *it* or *these* without having to name them explicitly for the other interactants.

Another difference lies in the overall structure of written and spoken texts. Written texts are products which have particular beginning, middle and end structures depending on the type of text, or genre, they are. For example a recount retelling the sequence of events in a traffic accident will, typically, have the structure:

1 **Orientation:** information on the context of the event
2 **Record of Events:** a record of the events as they occurred in sequence
3 **Reorientation:** closure or a conclusion to the events

The structure of written texts is relatively fixed and is determined by our cultural expectations of how the type of text we are writing typically unfolds. It is generally possible for readers to predict quite easily how the text is likely to be structured. Spoken texts, on the other hand, are more open-ended and dynamic, and may be much more closely tied to the actions occurring in the immediate context, with one utterance leading to another as we saw in the earlier examples of unscripted spoken language. Casual conversations also often range over a number of different topics as the speakers interact but some segments of casual conversation, such as when someone is telling an anecdote or recounting events, can exhibit an obvious

beginning, middle and end structure (Slade 1990). Speech is dynamic, therefore it is much more difficult for the speakers to predict the exact direction the interaction will take.

The different situations in which spoken and written texts are produced give rise to a further linguistic difference. As written texts are not tied to the immediate context, they can be drafted and redrafted until the writer produces a final and polished version. In contrast, spoken texts must be produced as the speaker proceeds, and as a result that speech is full of hesitations, repetitions, overlaps and incomplete clauses. It is this feature of speech that underlies the view that speaking is ungrammatical. However, it is not so much the case that speech is ungrammatical but that speech and writing are grammatical in different ways. Halliday (1989) suggests that written language is characterised by its lexical density while spoken language has a greater degree of grammatical intricacy. To illustrate this, consider the following text; the first two are examples of spoken language, the third is an excerpt from a written report. (Hammond et al 1992: 6):

Text A

X: Can I <u>come</u> and <u>show</u> you?
Y: Yes, OK
X: I've <u>finished</u> with this <u>bit</u>. Do you think <u>that</u> should <u>go</u> here?
Y: Yeah, that's <u>fine</u>.

Text B

<u>Colleagues worked</u> on the <u>task</u>. <u>Sue wrote</u> the <u>introduction</u>. <u>Jenny wrote</u> the <u>body</u> of the <u>article</u> and then they <u>edited</u> it. They <u>made sure</u> that the <u>two parts</u> were <u>consistent</u> in <u>style</u>.

Text C

<u>The completion</u> of the <u>document</u> was <u>achieved</u> through the <u>collaborative participation</u> of <u>colleagues</u>. The <u>editing process necessitated ensuring consistency</u> of <u>style</u> between the <u>various segments</u> of the <u>document</u>.

In these three texts the lexical or content items have been underlined but not the grammatical or structural words. We can see that as the texts move further from the shared physical context in Text A, the number of lexical items increases. We can think of spoken and written language as existing on a continuum with the most concrete 'here and now' spoken texts at one end and the most formal and abstract written texts at the other. The more written the text, the greater the lexical density becomes, as in Text C. This is because more information is being packed into Text C by the writer because the text has to recreate the situation for the reader at a distance, in a way that the spoken Text A does not have to do for the listener. Text A has few lexical items than Text C, but is more grammatically intricate, with clauses being added on one after the other as the speakers create the text together.

To explore the grammatical differences between speech and writing a little further, we need to introduce the related idea of nominalisation. Halliday (1985) suggests that nominalisation is to do with the process of changing actions into things, in other words changing language which is normally expressed as verbs into nouns; for example *condense* becomes *condensation*. We can see how this occurs by comparing the three sample texts.

Texts A and B	Text C
subjects of the clauses are typically the people who carry out the action: I, you, colleagues, Sue, Jenny, they	nominalisation occurs
	subjects of the clauses are not people, but happenings expressed as nouns: the completion of the document, the editing process
actions they complete are realised as verbs: come, show, finished, go, worked, wrote, edited	other parts of the clauses are also nominalised: the collaborative participation of colleaques, consistency of style, the various segments of the document

In Text C the lexical items have been combined into longer units of meaning known as nominal groups (eg *the completion of the document* and *the collaborative participation of colleagues*. Eggins (1994: 60) defines the nominal group as 'the part of the clause that contains nouns and the words that can accompany nouns'. Because nominal groups allow more content information to be packed into the written text, Text C becomes shorter and denser than Text B. Nominal groups also allow us to increase the amount of information carried in the one sentence.We could, for example, continue to put more information into Text C by extending the nominal groups as shown in the boxed example below.

---

the various segments of the document
the various relevant segments of the document
the various relevant segments of the policy document
the various relevant segments of the new policy document
the various relevant segments of the new policy document which was released yesterday

---

TASK 1.6

1 Read the three texts below and underline the nominal groups.
2 Trace how nominalisation has taken place from one text to the other.

Text A

Mother: It's so hard to choose isn't it … do you think she'd like these?
Father: Well, they're OK … but these bits at the side look as though they could come off pretty …
Mother: I see what you mean...what if she swallowed them and...
Father: Well, if he gets his hands on them, they'd be gone in two minutes, you …
Mother: OK, I've decided … it's the other ones. These aren't safe enough …

Text B

These days, when parents buy toys for their young children, they have a huge range from which to choose. Manufacturers now offer vast numbers of educational and leisure products in a great variety of stimulating and colourful materials. However, mothers and fathers still need to be cautious about whether these toys are safe for young children. Many of the cheaper toys have parts which are not well fitted. They can sometimes cut children if they are pulled off, or they may be small and easily swallowed.

Text C

In contemporary society, the parental purchase of pre-school children's toys has become a complex process of selection from a very substantial quantity of available products. Despite the immense assortment obtainable, considerable caution still needs to be exercised, particularly in relation to the materials used and the construction of these products, as there may be potential physical threats to the child's safety.

A summary of the general differences

Spoken and written language serve different social purposes and therefore have different characteristics. They both draw on the same vocabulary and grammatical resources of the language but they utilise them in different ways (Halliday 1989; Hammond et al 1992). Table 1.1 summarises the general differences between spoken and written language.

Table 1.1 Comparisons between spoken and written language

Spoken language	Written language
Context dependent	*Context independent*
• generally used to communicate with people in the same time and/or place	• used to communicate across time and distance
• relies on shared knowledge between the interactants and often makes reference to the shared context	• must recreate for readers the context it is describing
• generally accompanies action	• generally reflects action
Dialogic in nature	*Monologic in nature*
• usually involves two or more speakers creating spoken texts together	• usually written by one person removed from an audience
Unrehearsed and spontaneous but not unpredictable	*Edited and redrafted*
• interactants build spoken, unrehearsed texts spontaneously within social and linguistic parameters	• written language can be edited and redrafted any number of times
Records the world as happenings	*Records the world as things*
• relies more on verbs to carry meaning	• relies more on nouns and noun groups to carry meaning
Grammatically intricate	*Lexically dense*
• tends to contain more content or grammatical words such as pronouns, conjunctions etc	• tends to contain more lexical or content words as meaning is carried by nouns and noun groups
• develops through intricate networks of clauses rather than complete sentences as it is jointly constructed and relies more heavily on verbs	• relies on the process of nominalisation whereby things which are not nouns can be turned into nouns

Spoken and written language working together

In some social contexts spoken language is used as the dominant form of communication, for example, when we communicate with our families. In other contexts we use both spoken and written, for example in educational contexts – although in this context written language is given more status.

Over recent years there has been an increasing amount of research into the uses people make of language in everyday situations. This research has shown that in many social situations spoken and written texts work together. Let's consider the spoken and written texts involved in a meeting at work:

Receive notice of meeting in pigeon-hole	Telephone chairperson to request item be placed on agenda	Agenda sent out two days before meeting	Call for apologies	Minutes of previous meeting read	Minutes accepted	Discussion of agenda items one by one	Writing of minutes

The sequence of spoken and written texts will vary in different work contexts; however the sequence outlined in our example illustrates how spoken and written texts can operate side by side in a context. It is therefore important in teaching programs that we enable students to develop both spoken and written skills as they will need both to operate effectively in many social situations. In terms of program planning, this issue is addressed in Chapter 4.

Implications for teaching

Understanding the characteristics of spoken and written language and the linguistic similarities and differences is helpful for language teachers. Thinking about these features enables us to consider:

- the different situations in which spoken and written language are produced and how this affects the linguistic choices available to writers and speakers
- how we can select appropriate materials for teaching speaking according to the kinds of contexts learners find themselves in and the kind of speaking interactions they may have to negotiate
- whether scripted dialogues are always going to be appropriate for our learners' needs or whether we may need to introduce them to real samples of spoken data
- teaching materials available for teaching speaking and look critically at whether they reflect the real characteristics of spoken language.

Assisting learners to develop strategies for understanding the nature and processes of spoken language is an important teaching goal. It will involve helping learners to understand that:

- speaking is an active process of negotiating meaning and of using social knowledge of the situation, the topic and the other speaker
- speaking does not always mean using grammatically complete and written-like sentences
- speaking strategies differ depending on the purpose of the interaction

- transactional and interactional spoken texts have different features and require different skills
- speakers jointly develop the text and to identify some of the likely ways that a spoken interaction may be structured or may unfold.

Throughout this book we take a perspective on the teaching of speaking which is based on understanding the features of spoken discourse and how spoken discourse is used in everyday life. We do this because we believe that there is now a growing interest in applied linguistics generally in the development of curriculum approaches and teaching materials for second
language learning which introduce learners to language as it is actually used for real communicative purposes.

REVIEW

In this chapter we have focused on the following issues in relation to the nature of spoken language:

- Speaking is more than just a way of making conversation; we use spoken language for a variety of reasons in daily life.
- We exchange meanings through spoken language.
- Being a speaker also involves being a listener and these two skills are complementary and both actively help to create meaning.
- Learners need to be able to examine real examples of interaction as well as idealised dialogues.
- Spoken language is different from written language and has its own systematic patterns and language forms.
- Spoken texts and written texts often occur within one social situation and work together to form meanings within that situation.

References

Brown, G. and G. Yule. 1983. *Discourse analysis.* Cambridge: Cambridge University Press.

Eggins, S. 1994. *An introduction to systemic functional linguistics.* London: Pinter.

Halliday, M.A.K. 1975. *Learning how to mean: Explorations in the development of language.* London: Edward Arnold.

Halliday, M.A.K. 1994. *An introduction to functional grammar,* 2nd ed. London: Edward Arnold.

Halliday, M.A.K. 1985. *Spoken and written language.* Victoria: Deakin University Press.

Hammond, J., A. Burns, H. Joyce, D. Brosnan and L. Gerot. 1992. *English for social purposes.* Sydney: NCELTR.

McCarthy, M. 1991. *Discourse analysis for language teachers.* Cambridge: Cambridge University Press.

Slade, D. 1990. The analysis of spoken data. Paper presented at the NCELTR Spoken Discourse Project Workshop, September.

Anderson, A. and T. Lynch. 1988. *Listening.* Oxford: Oxford University Press.

Further reading   Burns, A., H. Joyce and S. Gollin. 1996. *'I see what you mean.' Teaching spoken discourse in the classroom: A handbook for teachers.* Sydney: NCELTR.

Bygate, M. 1988. *Speaking.* Oxford: Oxford University Press.

Carter, R. and McCarthy, M. (forthcoming). *Speaking English.* Cambridge: Cambridge University Press.

Cook, G. 1989. *Discourse.* Oxford: Oxford University Press.

Eggins, S. and D. Slade. 1997. *Analysing casual conversation.* London: Cassell.

Hammond, J. 1990. Is learning to read and write the same as learning to speak?. In Christie, F. (ed). *Literacy for a changing world.* Melbourne: ACER.

McCarthy, M. and Carter, R. 1994. *Language as discourse: Perspectives for language teaching.* London: Longman.

CHAPTER TWO

PRODUCING AND NEGOTIATING SPOKEN LANGUAGE

PREREADING QUESTIONS Closely observe (or if possible record) yourself taking part in a spoken interaction and answer the following questions:

- In what kind of social context did the interaction take place?
- Who took part?
- Was the interaction mainly transactional or interactional?
- What kinds of strategies did you use to:
  - get involved in the interaction
  - build up the points you wanted to exchange with the other speakers
  - ensure that your message was being understood?
- What kind of social and linguistic knowledge did you use to understand how the interaction was likely to proceed?

In Chapter 1 we touched on the nature of spoken language and the differences between speech and writing. In order to understand more about what happens when people are involved in spoken interactions, we need to consider the following two aspects of speaking which occur simultaneously:

- the production of language and how this affects the way speakers draw on their language resources to say things in different contexts
- the negotiation of meaning between speakers and the kinds of discourse strategies they employ in order to get their meanings across.

In this chapter we will consider some of the key linguistic features of production and negotiation in speaking, and then, for each feature, highlight the implications for teaching and classroom activities.

The production of language

In Chapter 1 we suggested that there are a number of significant differences between situations where spoken language is produced and ones where written language is the dominant mode. The most important factor is that spoken language is normally spontaneous. Speakers have less time to plan than writers and they often have to produce what they want to say on the run. This time restriction creates constraints on the speakers' processing of language and gives rise to a number of linguistic devices which speakers use to maintain the flow of the interaction. In this section we discuss the following three features of production which have an impact on the kind of language speakers produce:

- parataxis and hypotaxis
- formulaic expressions
- ellipsis

It is helpful for teachers to be aware of how these features operate in native speaker talk as this can assist in understanding that processing constraints operate for native speakers as well as for learners of the language. Devising classroom activities which promote the use of parataxis and hypotaxis, formulaic expressions and ellipsis may actively contribute to helping learners speak English more easily as well as enabling their language production to sound more natural.

Parataxis and hypotaxis

One way in which speakers are able to quickly produce the messages they wish to share is by building up a series of continuing elements of information as they talk. To do this they use coordinating conjunctions such as *and* and *but* to produce clauses which are independent of one another. The relationship between independent clauses is called *parataxis* (Halliday 1985) and in the following example the two clauses are related paratactically (‖ = clause boundary):

> So we went to the beach ‖ and had a picnic.
> We wanted to have a picnic at the beach ‖ but it was raining.

This is a different relationship to *hypotaxis* in which the subordinate clause cannot stand alone but is dependent on the main clause (Halliday 1985). The following is an example of hypotactically related clauses in spoken language. The clauses are related hypotactically because the second is dependent on the first:

> So we decided to go to the beach ‖ 'cause it was so hot.

As we suggested in Chapter 1, written language is generally more lexically dense than spoken language, and considerably more content information is packed into a written text. Avoiding the process of nominalisation and the long nominal groups which are more typical of written texts allows speakers to relieve the pressure to produce their meanings quickly. However, by adding information to the interaction through hypotactic and paratactic clauses, they produce language which is grammatically intricate.

Task 2.1

Read the following text and answer the questions.

1 What instances of parataxis are there?
2 What instances of hypotaxis are there?
3 How frequently does parataxis occur compared with hypotaxis?
4 To what extent does Kate use nominalisation or nominal groups in her talk?

The speaker, Kate, is putting forward her point of view in a student discussion in a university tutorial group. The clauses in the text have been marked.

What Melissa was saying ‖ about how someone actually puts a book out ‖ … and then you know … ‖ they become more powerful and more powerful ‖. It's like the cultures in society … ‖ A culture takes over. ‖ The British culture came out here ‖ and a lot of European cultures came ‖ and joined it … ‖ and it was strong enough ‖ to take over the Aboriginal culture ‖ and thus it is seen to take over … ‖ it's seen as an expert, ‖ it's more powerful ‖ and so it's treated thus … ‖ and so the levels on which the different cultures are based on ‖ … I suppose ‖ are interpreted as being a larger margin ‖ as the years have gone by … ‖ and it's only now ‖ that we are trying ‖ to start ‖ to bring the margins back together again, ‖ but it's gone at such a phenomenal rate … ‖ you know, ‖ that it's backtracking … ‖ and it's going ‖ to take a very long time.

We can see that in her contribution to the seminar discussion Kate employs parataxis (eg 'and a lot of European cultures came') much more than hypotaxis (eg 'that it's backtracking'). She also mainly uses the coordinating conjunctions 'and' and 'but', and there are only a few nominal groups (eg 'British culture', 'European culture').

Implications for teaching

We can use the concepts of parataxis and hypotaxis in speech production to help language students to understand how speakers typically build up their speech by linking a series of informational elements through commonly used conjunctions. Depending on the level of the learners, classroom strategies for teaching could include:

- discussing with learners the different ways in which spoken and written language connect pieces of information
- using samples of natural speech by native speakers from different contexts in recorded and/or transcribed forms
- providing listening exercises where learners can listen to the way talk is segmented into informational chunks
- encouraging learners to note how informational units are linked and what conjunctions are used
- giving learners practice in producing extended stretches of talk where they put forward a point of view or recount a series of events over a prolonged turn at talk.

We can also think about how we can increase the length of the turns that students are given in classroom interactions. Usually teachers only allow a short amount of wait time before they supply answers to their own questions, continue the interaction on behalf of students, or call on other students. Providing students with more time for classroom turns may help them to practise the linguistic devices of parataxis and hypotaxis required for more extended speech.

Formulaic expressions

Another way speakers facilitate spoken language production is by the use of formulaic expressions. These are set expressions, idioms or colloquialisms which are typically used by speakers over and over again in very familiar situations. They are expressions which are made up of wordings which are fixed or tend to go together and which over time have become widely accepted as conventional ways of saying certain things. For instance, if we want to tell someone about unexpectedly encountering a mutual acquaintance we have not seen for a while, we might use a common expression such as *You'll never guess who I just met!* Other examples of common formulaic expressions are:

Don't mention it
Hi there, how're things going?
Can I get you something to drink?
I don't want to put you to any trouble
It's my shout; have this one on me.
Have your heard the one about …
Could I have a word with you?

Speakers find these expressions particularly helpful in routine situations where they are relaxed, or not under pressure to create new structures of language, and can rely on well-recognised pieces of language to speed up and smooth social interactions. Formulaic expressions are very common in the opening and closing sequences of interactions where speakers can rely on well-known conventional patterns for what are often very routine situations.

TASK 2.2

Read the following text and underline the formulaic expressions that the two women use (one has been done for you).

In this text Sarah (S) is just coming to the end of a conversation with the mother of her friend, David (M). It is the first time the two women have met and Sarah, who is from America, is giving David's mother her impressions of Australia.

S: I saw signs with a kangaroo and a koala bear on it … and obviously I'm not used to that … it was great! I went out and took pictures of it.

M: You didn't see the real kangaroos or the real koalas.

S: We saw real koalas.

M: Did you?

S: Yeah … up in the trees.

M: You were very lucky.

S: Yeah, that's what I've been told. Yeah. That's very exciting. I still haven't seen a kangaroo yet, but considering I've been around Sydney, I don't really expect to see one for a while.

M: Yeah. Well, I hope you enjoy your stay here.

S: Thank you.

M: Nice talking to you.

S: Thanks. You too.

Both Sarah and David's mother introduce a number of formulaic expressions into their conversation:
• Sarah uses common expressions for giving positive evaluations of things or experiences (eg 'it was really great', that's very exciting').
• David's mother uses an expression to evaluate Sarah's experience ('You were very lucky).

- Sarah responds with a further formula ('That's what I've been told).
- Both speakers also use formulaic expressions to end the conversation (eg 'Well, I hope you enjoy your stay here' and 'Nice talking to you'.)

Implications for teaching

When learning a new language, formulaic expressions are frequently the elements of language which learners learn first. They are the survival aspects of the language which allow them to begin practising their new speaking skills. They are also, as we have suggested, a common tool employed by native speakers to assist them with spoken language production, and it is valuable for teachers to be aware of situations where formulaic expressions are commonly used and to explicitly teach these expressions to learners. We can encourage learners to practise using these formulaic expressions as part of a repertoire of language devices that aid them in routine situations and contexts. Classroom strategies for teaching formulaic expressions could include:

- practising common expressions for initiating and closing interactional casual conversations (eg chatting to neighbours)
- practising common expressions for initiating and closing transactional interactions (eg going to the bank)
- identifying formulaic expressions which are frequently used in casual conversation (eg talking about the weekend's activities)
- identifying formulaic expressions which are frequently used in transactional interactions (eg enquiring about the purchase of goods)
- practising expressions which assist the negotiation of meaning (eg asking for clarification, repetition, confirmation)
- teaching formulaic expressions which facilitate classroom interaction (eg requesting materials).

Ellipsis

The use of ellipsis also eases the pressure to produce spoken language. Ellipsis involves omitting parts of structures which would usually be required by the grammar. It is done on the assumption that the listener can understand what the speaker is referring to because of their shared knowledge of the context and because of the proximity of previous grammatical structures. For example, if a speaker asks, 'Where's Doug?', we are more likely to reply, 'In the bath', rather than 'Doug is in the bath'. In fact, our listeners would probably think we were being rather stilted and overly formal if we produced complete utterances in reply to some questions.

Speakers commonly condense their responses through ellipsis as a way of reducing what might be unnecessary information. In order to do so they make a judgement about what will be obvious to the listener. If these judgements are not correct then a breakdown in communication may occur as the listener fails to comprehend what the speaker is referring to.

Read the following text and answer the questions.

1 What shared cultural and social knowledge are the speakers assuming?
2 What examples of ellipsis can you find in their discussion?
3 Are there other ways in which language is abbreviated?

In this text, Pippa (P) and Vic (V) are exchanging information about the Festival of Sydney which occurs annually in January.

P: … I just saw the Herald there.

V: Did you?

P: Um … Today's the Festival of Sydney … the big eighty page cover …

V: Oh, yes. I didn't. Saw something in the Tele. I think … about the plays … that are on …

P: Yes worth getting because it covers everything … and a lot is [free …

V: [Oh yes, yes

P: I love Sydney at that time …

Both speakers make assumptions about shared knowledge and use abbreviated forms of language. For example, the speakers are making a number of assumptions about shared cultural knowledge in their references to Sydney newspapers (Herald and Tele) and the fact that extensive information about the events of the Festival of Sydney is to be found in these papers. They use ellipsis to make grammatical abbreviations (eg 'Did you?', 'I didn't', 'Saw something', 'Worth getting', 'a lot is free' rather than *Did you see it? I didn't see it. I saw something about it, a lot of the events are free*). There is also another abbreviated form in the contraction 'didn't' which is used because the language is conversational and informal.

Implications for teaching

Learners, particularly those who have previously learned language through formal written dialogues or through completing written exercises, may have had little exposure to ellipsis in English. Language teaching has had a tendency to encourage students to answer questions in complete sentences, and written exercises have often demanded complete sentence responses.

This emphasis on whole sentences is understandable because teachers have generally wanted their students to learn complete grammatical structures. However, in some instances it may be more appropriate, as well as more helpful, to allow students to answer in the abbreviated forms we have already discussed. For example, in tasks which focus on fluency rather than on accuracy, we can give students the opportunity to practise using ellipsis so that they sound less formal.

It is likely that the concept of ellipsis will be familiar to many learners from their own languages. However, the grammatical structures and forms which realise ellipsis may differ and we may need to teach these explicitly in English. Classroom strategies for teaching ellipsis could include:

- discussing the notion of shared knowledge and redundancy in contexts
- making comparisons between the use of ellipsis in first language and in English
- using real samples of spoken interaction to provide examples of how native speakers use ellipsis
- teaching language forms which involve ellipsis (eg verb ellipsis, pronoun ellipsis, clause ellipsis)
- providing oral exercises which practise patterns of ellipsis (eg language drills)
- encouraging learners to answer questions with abbreviated structures where appropriate.

The negotiation of meaning

The second aspect of speaking considered in this chapter is the negotiation of meaning which must occur dynamically as spoken interactions proceed. That is, speakers must not only cope with the processing constraints of time, they must also manage the interaction so that meanings are successfully exchanged with others.

Negotiation operates at the macro level and the micro level. At the macro level, speakers draw on their knowledge about the typical stages or phases that are likely to occur in different interactional contexts. At the micro-level, they draw on knowledge of, for example, how and when to take turns appropriately, how to clarify misunderstandings, how to keep the interaction on track, how to rephrase and how to provide feedback to the other speaker. In this section we look at three of these negotiation features - the first at the macro level and the other two at the micro level. These are:

- overall discourse structure
- turn taking
- topic management.

Overall discourse structure

As we suggested in Chapter 1, spoken interactions fall into two broad categories – transactional and interactional. Transactional situations usually involve people in interactions where they wish to obtain information or goods and services. Going to the bank to obtain a new credit card, phoning a library for information about joining or being interviewed for a job are all examples of transactional interactions. Interactional situations usually involve speakers in casual conversations where the main purpose is to establish or maintain social contact with other people. Examples include talking to old friends over a meal, chatting to your son's new school friend and talking to your partner after work. The language we choose to use in these conversations will be affected by a number of variables such as how well we know the other speakers, how often we speak to them, how we feel about them and how we judge our relative status. Although many interactions are a mixture of both, it is helpful for teaching purposes to be able to classify speaking activities broadly in this way.

As their experience of spoken interaction within their culture develops, native speakers learn the typical patterns which characterise different social interactions and use this knowledge to predict how talk is likely to unfold and to make broad predictions about the different stages and patterns an interaction will follow. Native speakers know how interactions are likely to begin, how they will continue and how they may end. We refer to these typical structurings of interactions as genres (Martin 1989).

Transactional interactions

If we take the service encounter as an example of a transactional genre we can examine how this genre is staged. Ventola (1987) suggests that in most service encounters in shops in Western cultures the following structure is common (^ = followed by):

Offer of service ^ Request for service ^ Transaction ^ Salutation

We can see this structure in Table 2.1 which is a service encounter between a shopkeeper (S) and a customer (C) (adapted from Ventola 1987: 3).

Table 2.1: Structure in a service encounter

Interaction	Structure
S: Yes please [rising tone]	Offer of service
C: [C turns to S] Six stamps, please	Request for service
S: [getting stamps and handing them over the counter] A dollar twenty. [C hands over a $20 dollar note to S] S: Thank you, twenty dollars [hand ing over the change] It's a dollar twenty that's … two, four, five, ten, and ten is twenty. Thank you.	Transaction
C: Thanks very much	Salutation

The language that speakers actually use in such encounters will vary from situation to situation, but the underlying patterns of many kinds of interactions, particularly transactional interactions, are largely predictable. This is not to suggest that they are rigidly fixed, but rather that there are recognisable stages which will unfold as the speakers negotiate a particular transactional interaction.

List the typical stages or patterns that occur in the following situations:

- consulting a general practitioner
- having a job interview
- ordering a meal in a restaurant
- checking into a hotel

Interpersonal interactions

Casual conversations, or interpersonal interactions, are generally less easy to predict than transactional interactions because they tend to be more open-ended and involve more frequent shifts in topic. Nevertheless, they generally have broad elements of predictable structure embedded in them as shown in Table 2.2.

Table 2.2: Structure in a conversation

Opening stages	beginnings (eg salutations and greetings such as *Hello, How are you)*
	initiating exchanges which establish social relations (eg formulaic expressions such as *How're things, What've you been up to since I last saw you*)
Middle stages	development of a wide range of topics
Ending stages	pre-closing exchanges signalling the ending (eg discourse markers and formulaic expressions such as *Anyway, Well, I'd better be off, Thanks for calling*)
	closings (eg formulaic expressions such as *Bye, See you*)

Once the intent to engage in a casual conversation has been established and initial greetings are completed, speakers are likely to cover a broad range of topics. Recent linguistic analysis of casual conversation (Slade 1997 and Eggins and Slade 1997) has revealed that it comprises two types of sequences:

1 Highly interactive sequences during which there is a rapid transfer of turns from one speaker to another and no speaker has an extended turn at talk. Slade (1997) refers to these segments as *chat*.

2 Sequences in which a speaker or a number of speakers hold the floor for an extended turn at talk. Slade (1997) refers to these segments as *chunks*. These chunk segments display patterns of internal structuring which are not found in the chat segments of casual conversation These authors have used generic structure analysis to identify the commonly recurring chunk segments of casual conversation.

Although stages in casual interaction are less easy to predict than those in transactional texts, it is still possible to identify the range of possible conversational genre types. Slade (1990) has pointed out that the genre types in casual conversation can be ordered along a continuum from those that display a clear generic structure at the left hand end to the non-generically structured segments (chat) at the other end as shown in Figure 2.1.

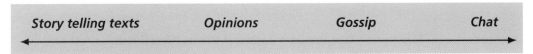

| *Story telling texts* | *Opinions* | *Gossip* | *Chat* |

Figure 2.1 Continuum of genre types in casual conversation

Slade suggests that at the story telling end of the continuum it is much easier to identify the unfolding stages or patterns; for example, a typical narrative will have various stages, some of which are obligatory if the text is to be considered a narrative, and some of which are optional. The typical stages of a narrative in spoken language as identified by Labov and Waletzky (1967) are set out below, with optional stages placed in parentheses (^ = followed by):

(Abstract) ^ Orientation to the events ^ Complication ^ Evaluation ^ Resolution ^ (Coda)

McCarthy and Carter (1994: 33) gloss these stages of the spoken narrative as follows:

Abstract	What is the story going to be about?
Orientation	Who were the participants? When and where did the action take place? In what circumstances?
Complicating action	Then what happened? What problems occurred?
Evaluation	What is the point of the story? So what?
Resolution	How did events sort themselves out? What finally happened?
Coda	What is the bridge between the events in the story and the present situation of the narrative?

Slade and Eggins identify three other types of stories which are frequently told in casual conversation in English. These are outlined below, but see Slade (1997) and Eggins and Slade (1997) for a more detailed discussion of these different types of stories.

Anecdotes	**(Abstract) ^Orientation ^ Crisis ^ (Coda)** Anecdotes are similar to narratives in that they focus on a crisis, but they have no explicit resolution. The crisis is reacted to in some way (eg through expressions of amazement, frustration, embarrassment or humiliation).
Exemplums	**(Abstract) ^ Orientation ^ Incident ^ Interpretation ^ (Coda)** Exemplums are told to give an explicit message on how the world should or should not be, to reaffirm cultural societal values.
Recounts	**(Abstract) ^ Orientation ^ Record of Events ^ Reorientation ^ (Coda)** Recounts retell events which are sequenced in time order and have some kind of evaluation running through them. The point is to retell events and share the speaker's evaluation.

The chat segments of casual conversations can include 'sending up' language (language where speakers make fun of one another) and language accompanying action and are much more difficult to analyse for generic structure. These interactions are extremely interpersonally oriented and context dependent and speakers must rely on their understanding of each other and of the objects in the immediate context and on the assumed knowledge they share. Individual exchanges in these interactions become linked in a highly localised way.

Implications for teaching

The concepts of interpersonal and transactional genre types and the predictable staging of texts provide a valuable discourse perspective to language teaching. The concepts give us a framework for categorising the texts we wish to introduce to our learners and we can use our knowledge of their generic patterns to help learners increase their understanding of predictable stages. We can also explore with learners cross-cultural perceptions and examine to what extent there are similarities and differences in text staging in different languages. Some of the issues that might be discussed include:

- Do speakers from some cultures omit or add stages which English speakers would find unexpected?
- Do speakers from some cultures exchange greetings and close conversations in the same way and are social relations established by exchanging the same kinds of culturally accepted information?
- What kinds of topics do people typically introduce into casual conversations?

Classroom strategies for teaching discourse structure could include:

- discussing the social purpose of different kinds of genres
- using real samples of spoken genres through recordings and transcripts to provide examples of how texts are staged
- making comparisons between the staging of texts in first language and in English
- teaching language forms which may occur at different stages (eg discourse markers and formulaic expressions for openings and closings, past tense forms of action verbs for recounts, personal and relative pronouns for language in action)
- providing oral exercises which enable students to practise specific language patterns (eg giving observations and comments, giving opinions).

Turn taking

We will now turn to one of the micro-level aspects of negotiating spoken discourse – how speakers manage turns in an interaction. An examination of turn taking includes looking at such things as:

- how speakers move from one turn to the next
- the types of turns which are expected in response to other turns
- how speakers self-select or give up their turns to others
- what interruptions and overlaps occur.

When an interaction is very cooperative and mutually supportive there are likely to be few overlaps in turns. In contrast, overlaps in less cooperative situations may be frequent and the utterances quite short as speakers compete to gain and keep a turn. In the following exchange Brian (B) and Tony (T) compete for turns in a discussion about the production of a newsletter:

    B: I'd like to get our [own …
    T: [A glossy for us would be good too
    B: … I'd like to get our own so that maybe we can even
        put two together.

Bygate (1989: 39) suggests that handling turns in spoken interactions involves five abilities which are outlined in Table 2.3 and glossed with examples.

Table 2.3: Abilities required in successful spoken interactions

1 signalling that one wishes to speak	this involves using gesture, phrases or sounds (eg *Ummm, Well, Can I just say something here, Hang on a minute*)
2 recognising the right moment to speak	this involves recognising intonation signals such as falling intonation or changes of pace or volume, pauses or closing discourse markers (eg *so anyway, yeah*)
3 using one's turn without losing it before it is finished	this involves saying the right amount and getting to the point which may vary from culture to culture
4 recognising signals of other people's desire to speak	this may involve being aware fo gesture and body language and initiating phrases or sounds (eg *er, um*)
5 letting someone else have a turn	this may involve nominating another speaker linguistically (eg *What do you think? You know him, don't you?*)

Turn taking conventions will vary according to particular contextual situations and will depend on such factors as:
- the topic
- whether the interaction is relatively cooperative
- how well the speakers know each other
- the relative status of the speakers.

In some situations certain speakers are clearly given more right to speak than others. This is true of a teacher in a classroom, a judge in a court of law or speakers who are considered to have particular expertise in relation to the topic under discussion.

Speakers often indicate when they do not wish to take a turn, but are merely attending to the interaction through devices known as backchannels, such as *Uh-hu, Mm, Yes, Right*, and *Sure* (Yngve 1970). It is also not uncommon in turn taking for speakers to complete or echo each other's utterances as they build on each other's contributions to extend the topic further or to predict what will be said next.

One unit of organisation which is related to the management of turn taking is the adjacency pair (Schegloff and Sacks 1973) where certain turn types require and expect certain kinds of responses, for example question/answer; offer/acceptance; greeting/greeting; or apology/acceptance. Some adjacency pairs have relatively fixed combinations of responses (eg Bye – Bye; Merry Christmas – Merry Christmas). Others, however, will vary according to their function within the specific context and their role in different exchanges in the interaction; for example, *Thanks* could be a response to a statement of congratulation, a compliment, an offer, the giving of information or an apology and so on.

TASK 2.5

Read the following text and identify instances of:

- overlap
- backchannel
- bids for a turn
- giving up a turn to the other speaker
- adjacency pairs - inform/acknowledge - offer/acceptance - request/response

In this text Liz (L) is talking to the Receptionist (R) at the Art Gallery.

R: Good morning, Art Gallery, can I help you?

L: Hi! I'd just like some … information about what exhibitions you   [have on …

R: [Right..

L: Is there anything special on … at the moment?

R: Well, we just have an exhibition that started yesterday. That's the 'Magnum in Our Time' Exhibition … it's a photo   [journalists …

L: [Right …

R: ... exhibition ... and the Cooke and Hinde exhibition from New York is coming, er ... on the twenty-second of September ...

L: [Oh, yeah ...

R: [... and if you're a member of the society you'll get the information in the magazine ...

L: [No, no, I'm not..

R: [and it'll also inform you of things that are coming up at the Gallery, exhibitions and that kind of thing ...

L: Oh good ...

R: If you're interested I could send you one ...

L: Yes, that would be good ...

Implications for teaching

As we can see from the above discussion, efficient turn taking involves both linguistic and non-linguistic features, and different cultural groups may make different assumptions about what is acceptable in turn taking; for example, some cultures may tolerate a much higher degree of overlap or interruption than others. There may also be variations in how much a speaker is expected or allowed to say in an individual turn or in what degree of pause time or silence is acceptable between turns. Non-verbal communication, such as gaze, body position and facial gesture is another area which plays a role in turn taking and which may differ from culture to culture. Second or foreign language speakers who flaunt expected conventions of turn taking can sometimes be considered rude, and unintended breakdowns in communication may occur.

Although it is not easy to directly teach differences in cultural conventions, learners may gain insights from discussing some of the more obvious differences and cultural expectations. Teachers can also raise awareness of specific linguistic devices for gaining and keeping turns. Classroom strategies for teaching turn taking may include:
- discussing cultural non-verbal differences for getting, keeping and giving up turns
- having students observe samples of natural recorded or videoed data to focus on the turn taking strategies used by native speakers
- raising awareness of native speaker turn taking strategies through discussion and observation
- practising and discussing learner use of turn taking strategies through role plays or recordings
- practising linguistic structures for getting, keeping and giving up turns.

Topic management

The final aspect of negotiating meaning we will discuss is the way in which speakers manage the topic. We will consider how speakers deal with changes in the topic, maintain the topic and repair the interaction when misunderstandings occur.

During spoken interactions topics are introduced, taken up and changed as a joint activity among speakers. Topics which are put up for discussion by any one speaker are either developed further or lapse through a kind of mutual consent between the speakers involved. Discussion of a particular topic generally proceeds until a new topic is introduced and taken up. The introduction of a new topic places an obligation on other speakers to respond and to join the speaker in moving the topic forward. Casual conversations are particularly prone to rapid changes of topic as people engage in freer and more spontaneous interaction than is generally found in transactional talk.

McCarthy (1991: 69-70) points out that one of the key ways in which topics are developed lies in how speakers take up, repeat and modify the vocabulary selections of others in order to expand, develop or change topics. McCarthy refers to this as *relexicalisation*. We will use McCarthy's model to show how this occurs in the following transactional text. The topic management in the first fifteen lines of the text is outlined in Table 2.4.

An enquirer (E) is telephoning an immigration officer (IO) on behalf of a friend to find out how to sponsor a family member to the country.

1	E:	So the children want to sponsor their mother.
2	IO:	How old are the children?
3	E:	Well, the oldest one's about 20 or so … but they haven't been
4		here for very long. They've only been here for about six months …
5	IO:	I see and they've been told that they can't sponsor her because
6		they haven't been here long enough. Yeah … there's a two
7		year residency requirement if she's an aged parent. How old is she?
8	E:	I don't know how old she is …
9	IO:	If she's below 60 years of age and that … she'll have to be
10		put through the points test
11	E:	Um …
12	IO:	And if that's the case then there's no resident requirement.
13		However if she's an aged parent … that's 60 years for women
14		… then, there's the two years residency requirement.
15	E:	Sorry, I didn't quite get what you mean … if she's under 60 she
16		can apply under the normal points system?
17	IO:	Yes, they can sponsor her because she'll be put through the points test
18		and it will depend on her qualifications and her experience. OK?
19	E:	What happens if she's a typical middle eastern mother who doesn't
20		have any qualifications and experience because she's been a mother.

21	IO:	And she's ... um ... below 60.
22	E:	Yeah
23	IO:	Well, there's not much there for her. She can always apply but
24		the likelihood of her being accepted would be greatly limited
25		... um ... that's one of the main problems there ... So, that's ...
26	E:	So after two years she can be sponsored by the children and their
27		sponsorship will be effective because they've been here for two years.
28	IO:	Well they can try sponsoring her now if she's below 60 ... uh ... if she
29		has to go through the points test, er, but you never know she may pass
30		the points test. You never know what her qualifications are.
31	E:	What kind of qualifications does she need to pass the points test?
32	IO:	Um, a trade certificate ... like say she's a qualified hairdresser for
33		instance and she's got years of experience ... we recognise that.

(From data collected during the NCELTR Spoken Discourse Special Project, 1995)

Table 2.4: Topic management of transactional interaction with immigration text

Topic management	Line
E's first turn concludes his description of the circumstances of the family on whose behalf he is enquiring and summarises the specific nature of of his enquiry (ie sponsorship)	1
IO shifts to the related topic of the age of the children	2
E relexicalises the topic of the children's ages as 'oldest'	3
E then goes on to introduce the topic of length of residence through 'but they haven't been here for very long'	3-4
IO develops the sponsorship-residency link through: • repetition of sponsor • they haven't been here long enough • there's a two year residency requirement	5 6 6-7
The topic of age is repeated through the relexicalisations of • 'aged parent' • 'How old is she?' • 'I don't know how old she is ...' • 'If she's below 60 years of age'	7 7 8 9
IO then introduces the new sub-topic of the points test, which is again related to age and residency through the repetition of: • 'residency requirement' • 'under 60'	10 14 15

TASK 2.6

Read the sponsorship text again and trace the repetitions and relexicalisations of the vocabulary to identify how the speakers expand the topic from Line 16 through the introduction of the new issues of qualifications and experience.

As well as introducing, developing and changing topics, speakers use a number of strategies to ensure that interactions proceed smoothly. Asking for clarification or repetition are ways of repairing an interaction when things become unclear. In the text above, E asks for clarification and repetition in two different ways:

- He indicates his need for clarification explicitly: 'Sorry, I didn't quite get what you mean' (Line 15).
- He uses the clarification technique of summarising what he has understood so far: 'So after two years she can be sponsored by the children and their sponsorship will be effective because they've been here for two years, (Lines 27–29). This technique achieves the result of encouraging the IO to provide more information .

Speakers will also sometimes use repetition and clarification when they sense that their message is not getting through to their listeners. This is often signalled explicitly with expressions such as: *What I was getting at was, I'm trying to tell you that, I'll just run over that again.*

Gatekeeping

Contexts such as the immigration enquiry recorded here can represent *gatekeeping* situations. These are situations where one speaker is in a more powerful position because they have access to information or to goods and services not available to the other speaker. In these situations speakers need to use negotiation strategies to ensure that they achieve the purpose of the interaction as fully as possible. One such strategy is to keep the interaction open when the other speaker tries to close it down. We can see examples of this in the immigration text where IO, having introduced the information about qualifications and experience, attempts to indicate to E that the interaction is coming to an end: 'OK?' (Line 18). E, however, is undeterred and uses the reference to qualifications and experience to extend the enquiry (Lines 19–21). He does this by introducing a hypothesis: 'What happens if she's a typical middle eastern mother ... ', which obliges IO to make a response. Four turns later, IO again tries to close the interaction with 'So that's ..., (Line 26) and again, E cuts off his attempt by using a clarification strategy to extend the enquiry (Lines 27–29). This time the clarification involves E in summarising his understanding of what he has been told so far. As we noted previously, this extension succeeds in reopening the topic and encourages IO to produce further information.

Implications for teaching

Casual conversations, where topics shift rapidly, are likely to be more problematic for second language learners than transactional interactions, where topic development is slower and more focused on detail. Culturally they are also more difficult because cultural expectations are involved in the choice of topics which can be raised in casual conversations between relative strangers. Discussing typical topics for casual conversation with learners and developing the associated vocabulary is one way of helping them to extend their interactional skills. Skills in topic development may also be increased by giving students tasks which extend understanding of vocabulary patterns such as synonyms, antonyms and other word associations. Drawing learners' attention to the way native speakers begin, develop or introduce a new topic, and the kind of language structures they use to do this can also be valuable.

Words and phrases for signalling requests for repetition or clarification can also be taught explicitly. As well as being useful outside the classroom, they can improve classroom interaction and give learners strategies for indicating when they have not understood. Classroom strategies for teaching topic management include:

- using samples of native speaker talk to focus on the kind of topics introduced in casual conversations in different contexts
- discussing the language patterns for introducing topics
- developing vocabulary related to different topics
- introducing and drilling word associations
- practising typical expressions for requesting clarification and repetition
- raising awareness of discourse strategies, such as summarising and hypothesising, in order to extend the interaction
- practising the linguistic structures for summarising and hypothesising.

REVIEW

This chapter has considered some of the key aspects of the production and negotiation of speech. For those who would like to explore this issue further, we provide a 'Further reading' list at the end of the chapter which offers more extensive discussion of these areas.

In this chapter we focused on three aspects of speech production: parataxis and hypotaxis, formulaic expressions, and ellipsis. We also considered three features of spoken texts which come into effect when speakers negotiate talk: overall discourse structure, turn taking, and topic management. The first of these involves negotiation at the macro-level of speech – as the name suggests – while the other two operate at the micro-level.

For each of these areas we discussed some of the implications for language teaching and made suggestions about the kinds of teaching strategies which could be explored in the classroom.

References

Bygate, M. 1987. *Speaking*. Oxford: Oxford University Press.

Eggins, S. and D. Slade. 1997. *Analysing casual conversation*. London: Cassell.

Halliday, M.A.K. 1985. *An introduction to functional grammar*. London: Edward Arnold.

Labov, W. and J. Waletzky 1967. Narrative analysis. In Helm, J. (ed). in *Essays on the verbal and visual arts*. Seattle: University of Washington Press: 12-14.

Martin, J. 1989. Types of writing in infants and primary school. Working with genre - Papers from the 1989 LERN Conference. Sydney: UTS.

McCarthy, M. 1991. *Discourse analysis for language teachers*. Cambridge: Cambridge University Press.

McCarthy, M. and R. Carter 1994. *Language as discourse: Perspectives for language teaching*. Harlow: Longman.

Schegloff, E. A. and H. Sacks. 1973. Opening up closings. *Semiotica*, 8(4), 289–327.

Slade, D. 1990. The analysis of spoken data. Paper presented at the NCELTR Spoken Discourse Project Workshop, Macquarie University, September.

Slade, D. 1997. The texture of casual conversation in English. PhD Thesis. Social Semiotics, University of Sydney.

Ventola, E. 1987. *The structure of social interaction: A systemic approach to the semiotics of service encounters*. London: Francis Pinter.

Yngve, V. H. 1970. On getting a word in edgewise. Papers from the 6th Regional Meeting, Chicago Linguistic Society. Chicago: Chicago Linguistic Society.

Further reading

Brown, G. and G. Yule. 1983. *Teaching the spoken language*. Cambridge: Cambridge University Press.

Burns, A., H Joyce and S. Gollin. 1996. *I see what you mean. Using spoken discourse in the classroom: A handbook for teachers*. Sydney: NCELTR.

Carter, R. 1987. *Vocabulary*. London: Allen and Unwin.

Cook, G. 1989. *Discourse*. Oxford: Oxford University Press.

Dalton, C. and B. Seidlhofer. 1994. *Pronunciation*. Oxford: Oxford University Press.

Gairns, R. and S. Redman. 1986. *Working with words*. Cambridge: Cambridge University Press.

Harmer, J. 1987. *The practice of English language teaching*. London: Longman.

Kenworthy, J. 1978. *Teaching English pronunciation*. London: Longman.

Leroy, C. 1995. *Pronunciation. Resource books for language teachers*. Oxford: Oxford University Press.

McCarthy, M. 1990. *Vocabulary*. Oxford: Oxford University Press.

Morley, J. (ed.). 1987. *Current perspectives on pronunciation: Practices anchored in theory*. Washington, D.C.: TESOL.

Nunan, D. 1993. *Introducing discourse analysis*. London: Penguin.

THREE

THEORETICAL PERSPECTIVES

Think about your own experiences of learning a second or foreign language.

- What kinds of activities did the teacher use to develop your speaking skills?
- What kinds of materials were used (eg course books, scripted dialogues, grammar exercises)?
- How similar or different are the activities you use in your own teaching of speaking?
- What beliefs do you have about teaching speaking to your learners? It may be helpful to think about this by listing your responses to the questions:
  - What do you think students should do to improve their speaking?
  - What do you think you should do to help students to improve their speaking?

Having examined the nature of spoken language in Chapters 1 and 2, we will now consider some theoretical approaches which have informed language teaching in the twentieth century and which have had various implications for the teaching of speaking. Language teaching has been influenced by, and has generally evolved from, linguistic theories and from theories of language acquisition and development. When considering current approaches to teaching speaking, it is helpful to understand these theories and how they have given rise to changes in the way second or foreign languages have been taught. Of necessity, the theoretical overview presented in this chapter is only a brief and selective introduction to this area. Further references are supplied at the end of the chapter for those readers interested in following up the issues discussed.

The grammar-translation method

The grammar-translation method emerged in response to a growing interest in the learning of foreign, generally European, languages in the nineteenth century. This method and other early approaches to language learning had their origins in the study of classical grammars such as Latin and Greek and the grammar-translation method continued to influence language teaching into this century. The focus in learning was on the knowledge of grammar and on applying this knowledge in the process of translating from one language to another. One of the central features of the method was the presentation of the new language through individual sentences which exemplified grammatical points. These points were presented one by one in an organised sequence, and sentences were specially constructed to provide understandable examples for the students. A typical lesson would include the presentation of a new grammatical point, a list of new vocabulary items to be learned and practice sentences for students to translate.

The grammar-translation method placed considerable emphasis on accuracy, although this did not necessarily mean accuracy in oral production, as exercises were generally read and written. This method also stressed the production of complete sentences. As the approach was based on written grammatical sources, the teaching of speaking was, in effect, neglected and teaching itself took place through the medium of the learner's first language. In fact, it was rare for the learner to hear the language being spoken other than for the purposes of translation.

This approach also encouraged a word-by-word construction of sentences, which ignored meaning and often produced unnatural sounding sentences. Natural spoken language was considered inferior to written language, being too formless and unstructured to be the subject of grammatical study. One of the main goals of this method was to develop skills that would allow learners to read the works of great literature or to experience the intellectual discipline of studying and analysing grammatical structure.

TASK 3.1

Look at Extract 1 from a book designed to teach Swahili to European settlers (Le Breton 1936: 26–7). What typical features of the grammar-translation approach are evident?

Extract 1 (Le Breton 1936)

VERBS ARE MADE PASSIVE by adding a -w- before the final vowel.

For euphony the passive termination sometimes becomes **-iwa** or **-ewa**, or when a vowel precedes the final **-a**, by **-liwa** or **-lewa**. Of this type the following verbs are among the commonest in general use.

Kuzaa	- To Give birth	**Kuzaliwa**	- To be Born
Kupima	- To Measure	**Kupimiwa**	- To be Measured or weighed
Kuchoma	- To Burn	**Kuchomiwa**	- To be Burnt (intentionally)

There is also a NEUTER FORM OF THE VERB, not unlike the passive, which is formed by changing the final -a into -ka, or for euphony into -ika. The following are the commonest of this type in general use.

TRANSLATE. — The child was beaten by the cook. The cords of the European's bundles were cut by the stranger and his companion. The water-jar has been upset by this fool and now has a hole in it. The honey is all spoilt, the child overturned the bucket and spilt the honey. What? Yes, the bucket was overturned and the honey was all spilt. When will the woman give birth? Sir, the child is already born. It is necessary to burn the skins of these tomatoes and has that paper been burnt?

The structural approach

In the first half of the twentieth century, the theories of American structural linguists such as Bloomfield (1933) and Fries (1945) gradually replaced the more traditional approaches of classical humanism, and the structural approach became influential in language teaching.

Structural linguists were interested in identifying and describing the basic grammatical forms and patterns of language within the sentence and categorising them objectively and scientifically. In terms of language teaching these categories were used to select and grade materials which illustrated the grammatical patterns and rules of the language and to provide practice in using them. Grammatical categories could also be used to contrast and compare different languages so that areas which might be potentially difficult for students could be predicted in advance.

The role of the teacher became somewhat secondary to the role of the materials in this approach, as mastery of the materials and the building up of knowledge of the grammatical structures was considered central. This assumption gave rise to the widespread use of language laboratories and teacher-proof course materials.

Structural linguists took the view that language learning involved constant practice and good habit formation. Learners were trained in correct speech-patterns and expected to practise them. There was a strong emphasis on repetition and on building up of linguistic items through drills and exercises which focused on grammatical structures and patterns. This approach coincided with the work of behavioural psychologists such as Watson (1924) and Skinner (1957) who emphasised the development of new habits of behaviour through a process of stimulus and response.

The Structural Approach attracted widespread interest and foreign language learning increased considerably in the 1940s and 1950s. It was an approach which gave a much greater emphasis to speaking than the previous grammar-translation method and new teaching approaches emerged, such as the audio-lingual method which involved introducing, in a fixed order, the four macroskills of language – listening, speaking, reading and writing. Student activities involved intense practice in aural-oral skills and focused on activities such as drills and substitution exercises taken from a graded syllabus. However, speaking skills focused exclusively on the development of correct grammatical utterances and good pronunciation. There was little interest in the contexts for speaking, which were used merely as a situational vehicle for the more important practice of grammar structure.

Transformational-generative linguistics

The theories of structural linguists were challenged in the 1950s and 1960s by Noam Chomsky who proposed that linguistic description should be concerned with the underlying mental systems humans used to generate sentences, rather than with describing fixed grammatical patterns. He referred to this underlying system as a *language acquisition device*. He believed that speakers of a language had mastered and internalised a system of rules and it was this knowledge which enabled them to transform language structures and to generate hypotheses about new language use; hence, the term *transformational-generative* was applied to Chomsky's theories of language.

Chomsky (1965) called this knowledge of language use *competence*, and contrasted it with *performance* which referred to the way language was actually used in social situations. His interest lay in the psychological dimension, that is in the mental competence or knowledge humans brought to language use, and he considered performance to be outside the scope of linguistic investigation.

His work did not give rise to a specific language teaching methodology; however, his views undermined the stimulus-response concepts of behavioural psychology and the audio-lingual approaches which emphasised the drilling and repetition of grammatical patterns. Their place was taken by an interest in cognitive methods which would enable language learners to hypothesise about language structures and grammatical patterns. There was also a growing recognition that learning was controlled by the learner rather than the teacher and that errors were an inevitable part of language learning. The teaching of explicit grammatical rules was seen as necessary, so that the learners could be prepared for practice in using the language creatively and innovatively.

Although cognitive approaches differed from audio-lingualism, which had focused on the memorisation of fixed language patterns and accurate reproduction, in the language teaching methods current in the 1960s and early 1970s acquiring spoken language was still seen as a building-block process in which certain structures and grammatical patterns needed to be acquired before others could be learned. The particular ways in which these linguistic items should be sequenced and graded, however, was much less certain. A major concern in language teaching at this time was to find the best method through which to acquire a new language.

Communicative competence and social views of language teaching

Chomsky's theories were able to account for the knowledge of grammatical rules that the ideal speaker-listener has about his or her language. However they did not explain how a speaker knows how to use those rules appropriately for the purposes of social interaction. In the early 1970s, the anthropologist and linguist, Dell Hymes, challenged Chomsky's ideas about linguistic competence by taking up the issue of the speaker's performance or language use. He put it succinctly in an article challenging Chomsky's views (Hymes 1971: 68).

There are rules of use without which the rules of syntax are meaningless.

It was Hymes who coined the term *communicative competence* in which he included not only linguistic knowledge, but also knowledge of the cultural and communicative systems available to the speaker, and their relationship with the setting, participants, purpose, channel of communication and topic.

From the 1970s the work of sociolinguists such as Hymes has influenced the development of what is known as the *communicative approach* to language teaching. The development of this approach involved a shift away from thinking that language form should be the main focus of language teaching to a consideration of what it means to use language for communicative purposes. Being able to use language to communicate appropriately within different social contexts is a key aim in the communicative approach to language teaching. Some of the main features of this approach are:

- the notion of contextualising language within social contexts rather than teaching language as a system of grammatical patterns
- a concern not only with language form but also with language function
- the selection of content on the basis of student needs
- a concern with all the four macroskills of language, rather than primarily with reading and writing
- a tolerance of learner errors as an inevitable aspect of language acquisition
- the encouragement of learner independence in learning
- the notion of the teacher as a facilitator of learning.

There have been a number of variations in the communicative approach to language teaching. Some of the early approaches in the 1970s were based on very detailed analyses of learner communication needs, particularly those required for various professional occupations (such as Richterich 1972 and Munby 1978).

Another approach, taken by Wilkins (1976), proposed that learners needed a common core of language notions and functions which would equip them for learning the more specific language requirements of their occupations. *Notions* refers to semantic-grammatical concepts such as time (past, future etc), location, frequency, dimension, quantity and so on. For example expressing time and frequency involves using particular tenses and adverbial clauses (eg I visited my grandfather three times a year). *Functions* involve the practical uses of language such as making requests, offering suggestions, asking for directions, making enquiries, giving advice and so on. For example, *Can you tell me how to get to the post office?* involves the function of asking for directions.

Wilkin's work resulted in a functional-notional approach to language teaching, though generally teaching materials and approaches have drawn more on the idea of functions than on both function and notion, perhaps because the concept of function is more easily understood and less abstract.

Look at Extracts 2 and 3 which are taken from the table of contents of two language teaching textbooks and answer the following questions:

1 What approaches to language teaching do they suggest?
2 What do they assume about language theory and learning objectives?
3 What do they assume about how learners will develop speaking skills?

Extract 2 (Stannard Allen 1959)

CONTENTS
Subject-matter of exercises
(Alphabetical Index at back)

Section	Exercise No.		Page
1	1-8	Countable and uncountable nouns	1
2	9-10	Negatives and questions	8
3	11-13	Possessive pronouns	9
4	14	"Self"	10
5	15	Adverb order	11
6	16-19	Pronouns, case of	13
7	20-21	Possessive case	17
8	22	Introduction to interrogatives	19
9	23	Telling the time	20
10	24-25	"Too" and "enough"	20
11	26-29	"Some" and "any"	22

Extract 3 (Commonwealth of Australia 1980)

UNIT 1

UNIT 1	**GREETING AND INTRODUCING**
	SAYING GOODBYE

KEY STRUCTURES

PART A	**GREETING**

HOW ARE YOU?

HOW IS YOUR WIFE (HOW'S)?

HOW ARE YOU GOING?

HOW IS YOUR JOB GOING? (HOW'S)

RESPONSES

GOOD, THANKS.

NOT BAD, THANKS

SHE'S WELL, THANKS

PART B	**INTRODUCING**

I'D LIKE YOU TO MEET …

THIS IS (MY) …

RESPONSES

HOW DO YOU DO?

HOW ARE YOU?

HELLO.

WHAT IS HIS/HER NAME? (WHAT'S)

One of the effects of the various teaching methodologies which have developed under the banner of the communicative approach to language teaching has been a tendency to take the emphasis away from teaching grammatical structures and to focus primarily on language use. This was never the intention of the communicative approach, but the need to teach the structures and forms of language alongside the functional uses of language has sometimes been overlooked, and this tendency has been reinforced by the materials that have been designed for communicative language teaching. In some cases materials appear to suggest that being able to form the grammatical structures of the language is in opposition to purposeful communication, as the following introduction to published teaching materials appears to imply (Keltner, Howard and Lee 1981: ix):

> Book 1 is aimed primarily at developing the listening and speaking skills of adults who have had little or no previous instruction in English so that they may communicate effectively in the…content areas…
> The units are situation-oriented, non-sequential and minimally structured. They should not be considered solely as grammar lessons. Their primary purpose is to develop immediately useable oral communication skills. The materials take the students beyond the level of merely knowing about the new language, beyond the ability to repeat memorized dialogues and beyond mechanical substitutions of one word or structure for another.

This extract also suggests a further unintended direction of communicative language teaching in its emphasis on developing the listening and speaking skills and oral communication skills of the learners. This overlooks the fact that the term *communicative* was intended to apply to the development of all four language skills. In a communicative framework it is important to consider how spoken and written language are interrelated in authentic situations of language use.

Genre-based approaches

In recent times some of the methodologies which developed from communicative language teaching have been criticised for failing to focus on grammar and vocabulary. At the same time the work of functional linguists such as Halliday (1973) has begun to influence the teaching of language in all sectors of education. Halliday and his colleagues have been interested in developing an educational linguistics which is based on a functional model of language (not be confused with the functional-notional approach to language teaching which was described earlier).

Functional linguists are interested in the functional aspects of language; that is, in the purposes to which language is put within different contexts of situation. Halliday (1985) suggested that speakers learn to use language in order to fulfil a number of social functions within social contexts of language use and in order to do so select from a variety of language forms according to:

- the field, or the topic of communication
- the tenor, or the relationship of the participants involved in the interaction
- the mode, or the channel of communication.

Halliday and other functional linguistics define language as a resource which people use to make meanings in social contexts. They also define language as a network of interrelated systems from which speakers draw in order to construct connected discourse rather than random sets of sentences. For Halliday, what speakers and listeners and readers and writers do with language needs to be seen in relation to what they want to achieve within social contexts rather than as something that they produce as a result of knowing formal linguistic rules. However, functional linguists also provide information about the ways in which grammar is connected to the social uses of language.

The work of Halliday and his colleagues has led to an explicit approach to language teaching which emphasises:

- the importance of language teaching and learning at the discourse, or whole text level, rather than restricting it to the sentence level
- the importance of understanding the differences in the structures and linguistic patternings of spoken and written texts
- the central role of context and the way in which language changes and is changed by the contexts in which it occurs
- the teaching of grammar in conjunction with the teaching of whole texts.

One particular approach which has developed from functional linguistics is the *genre approach* to teaching whole texts (Martin 1989; Cornish 1992). The genre approach to language teaching is concerned with teaching students how texts within certain cultures have evolved particular discourse structures to fulfil particular social functions. The genre approach was originally developed to teach writing in general education contexts and it has begun to influence the teaching of second language writing. Its relevance to the teaching of speaking is just beginning to be explored (eg Burns, Joyce and Gollin 1996).

The implications of discourse analysis for language teaching are still in the early stages (eg Cook 1989; McCarthy 1991; Burns, Joyce and Gollin 1996), and approaches to second language teaching based on functional linguistics are still being developed (eg Cornish 1992; Hammond et al 1992; Joyce 1992). However, discourse analysis and functional linguistics suggest some promising new directions for the teaching and learning of second language speaking. Analysis of the discourse structure and grammar of whole authentic spoken texts is also continuing to expand (eg Carter and McCarthy, forthcoming Eggins and Slade 1997) and this will inevitably inform the development of spoken language teaching.

Look at Extracts 4–6 taken from the introductions to published materials for language teaching.* What theories of language teaching and learning do they seem to suggest? What assumptions are made about the development of speaking skills?

Extract 4

[This set of materials] emphasises the presentation of whole texts in context. These texts include: spoken texts such as telephone enquiries or casual conversations; written texts such as reports, formal letters and instructions; diagrammatic texts such as maps and charts. Language interactions are presented in context, so that the students know something about the purpose of the communication, the circumstances and the people involved.

...Activities are designed to promote independent learning strategies, including self-assessment, as well as to provide opportunities to work independently and collaboratively with other students.

Extract 5

The exercises in this book have been devised over a period of eight years, and are the results of practical experience with classes of foreign adults, including students of Latin, Teutonic, Slavonic and Arabic origin. All the exercises have been tried out and found practicable, and I hope they will prove useful and valuable to many other teachers of English.

This book is an attempt to answer the foreign student's grammatical problems empirically and to give him a large number of appropriate exercises to practise them. An English schoolboy does grammar as an analytical exercise, but the foreign student needs to learn the mechanics of the language.

Extract 6

The course is for use in the classroom. The matching Students' Books are not intended for self study without a teacher. The course presents an aural/oral approach; that is to say, students are taught to hear (aural) and to speak (oral) the language correctly before reading or writing it.

Each Teacher's Book provides detailed suggestions for the aural/oral teaching and practice of the materials in forty different units...and provides the teacher with the following kinds of guidance: a treatment of teaching techniques; guidance on lesson planning; a graded section of the teaching of English pronunciation.

* *Sources appear at end of chapter.*

Implications of language teaching theories for teaching speaking

Various fields of theoretical research, including linguistics, sociology, psychology and anthropology, have made an impact on the development of new language teaching approaches and methodologies. Since the 1970s, communicative approaches have had a major influence on teaching and learning in many parts of the world. As Dubin and Olshtain (1986) have suggested, one of the major benefits of communicative language teaching is that it has brought about a more comprehensive view of teaching and learning.

However, this is not to imply that the communicative approach has been, or must be, universally accepted and

practised. In some countries the discussion about the relevance and appropriacy of communicative methods in meeting the needs and purposes of the learners is still fairly recent and this may be related both to local perceptions and practical considerations. In addition, good teaching is always a matter of evaluating new theoretical insights and subjecting them to the test of practical applications in the classroom.

Elements of all the theories and approaches discussed in this chapter are likely to be evident in the broad range of course design and teaching methodologies currently employed in the teaching of second or foreign language speaking. What is valuable is that teachers should have an understanding of the various theoretical and practical advances that have been made and that this knowledge becomes the basis for making informed decisions about teaching within the particular circumstances of the organisational program. It may also be the case that previous approaches can be productively incorporated into newer theoretical and practical insights. This is done most effectively when teachers can draw knowledgeably on a wide repertoire of teaching and learning strategies in order to meet the needs of their learners.

Principles for teaching speaking

Drawing on the discussion presented in Chapters 1 and 2, we can suggest some general implications for the teaching of speaking which form the basis of the principles we adopt in this book. These implications are that:

- learners need to understand the cultural and social purposes of spoken interactions, which may be broadly classified as transactional or interactional
- speaking involves an understanding of the way in which context influences the choices of language made
- speaking involves understanding that spoken texts differ from written texts in their grammatical patterns and discourse strategies
- speaking activities should focus on whole texts in context, rather than on sentence level grammatical constructions in isolation
- learning and practising vocabulary, grammatical structures and pronunciation should be related to contexts and lead to the use of whole texts
- spoken discourse types or texts can be analysed with learners for their typical structures and grammatical patterns.

REVIEW

In this chapter we have provided a brief overview of some of the major theoretical perspectives that have influenced or are beginning to influence the teaching of second or foreign language speaking. These have included:

- grammar-translation approaches, based primarily on the study of classical languages, which emphasised the learning of language through written forms
- structural approaches, which were influenced by behaviourist theories of language development and which gave rise to audio-lingual methods of imitation, repetition and response
- cognitive theory, which introduced the notion of innate language performance and the need to practise language structure as a basis for creative language use
- the influence of sociological and anthropological research which gave rise to an interest in the appropriate use of language in social contexts
- the development of communicative approaches based on the notion of communicative competence
- functional linguistic, genre analysis and discourse analysis theories which highlight the need for approaches which reflect actual language use and the linguistic features and structures involved.

References

Bloomfield, L. 1933. *Language*. New York: Holt Reinhart & Winston.

Burns, A., H. Joyce and S. Gollin. 1996. *'I see what you mean' Teaching spoken discourse in the classroom: A handbook for teachers*. Sydney: NCELTR.

Carter, R. and M. McCarthy (forthcoming). *Speaking English*. Cambridge: Cambridge University Press.

Commonwealth of Australia. 1980. *Talk back: Elementary*. Canberra: AGPS.

Chomsky, N. 1965. *Aspects of the theory of syntax*. Boston, Mass: MIT Press.

Cook 1989. *Discourse*. Oxford: Oxford University Press.

Cornish, S. 1992. *Community access curriculum guidelines*. Sydney: NSW AMES.

Dubin, F. and E. Olshtain. 1986. *Course design*. Cambridge: Cambridge University Press.

Eggins, S. and D. Slade. 1997. *Analysing casual conversation*. London: Cassell.

Fries, C. 1945. *Teaching and learning English as a foreign language*. Ann Arbor: University of Michigan Press.

Hymes. D. 1971. Competence and performance in linguistic theory. In R. Huxley and E. Ingram (eds). *Language acquisition: Models and methods*. London: Academic Press.

Halliday, M.A.K. 1973. Explorations in the functions of language. London: Edward Arnold.

Halliday, M.A.K. 1985. *An introduction to functional grammar*. London: Edward Arnold.

Hammond, J., A. Burns, H. Joyce, D. Brosnan, L. Gerot. 1992. English for social purposes. Sydney: NCELTR.

Joyce, H. 1992. Workplace texts in the language classroom. Sydney: NSW AMES.

Keltner, Howard, Lee. 1981. *English for adult competency*. Upper Saddle River: Prentice Hall.

Keltner A., L. Howard and F. Lee 1981. *Competency for English* New Jersey: Prentice Hall.

Le Breton, F.H. 1936. Up-country Swahili for the farmer, merchant, businessman,and their wives,and for all who deal with the up-country African. Richmond: R.W.Simpson and Co Ltd.

Martin, J. R. 1989. Types of writing in infants and primary school. In *Working with genre*. Papers from the 1989 LERN Conference, University of Technology, Sydney.

McCarthy, M. 1991. *Discourse analysis for language teachers.* Cambridge: Cambridge University Press.

Munby, J. 1978. *Communicative syllabus design.* Cambridge: Cambridge University Press.

Richterich, R. 1972. *A model for the definition of language needs of adults learning a modern language.* Strasbourg: Council of Europe.

Skinner, B. 1957. *Verbal behaviour.* New York: Apprelton Century Crofts.

Watson, J. 1924. *Behaviourism.* New York: Norton.

Wilkins, D.A. N*otional syllabuses: A taxonomy and its relevance to foreign language curriculum development.* Oxford: Oxford University Press.

Extract 4 from Cornish, S. and S. Hood, 1994. *Troubled waters: Teacher's Guide for beginner and intermediate levels 1 & 2.* Sydney. NSW AMES: viii.

Extract 5 from Stannard Allen, W 1959. *Living English structure.* London: Longmans: vii.

Extract 6 from Department of Education and Science for the Department of Immigration. 1969. *Situational English, Part 1 Teacher's Book.* London: Longman.

Further reading

Harmer, J. 1983. *The practice of English language teaching.* New York: Longman.

Howatt, A.P.R. 1984. *A history of English language teaching.* Oxford: Oxford University Press.

Richards, J.C. and T. Rodgers. 1986. *Approaches and methods in language teaching.* Cambridge: Cambridge University Press.

Stern, H.H. 1992. *Issues and options in language teaching.* Oxford: Oxford University Press.

Savignon, S. 1983. *Communicative competence: Theory and classroom practice.* Reading, Mass: Addison-Wesley.

Widdowson, H. G. 1990. *Aspects of language teaching.* Oxford: Oxford University Press.

FOUR

THE SPEAKING NEEDS AND GOALS OF LANGUAGE STUDENTS

PREREADING QUESTIONS

- How do you find out the needs and goals of your students in relation to speaking?
- How do you talk about your students' level of speaking?
- How do you go about planning to meet the needs of your students?

Language programs which aim to teach speaking

One of the aims of most of the language programs used by today's teachers is to develop spoken language skills, and most programs aim to integrate both spoken and written language. However, the emphasis given to speaking in a language program varies according to the needs and goals of the students and the focus of the course.

In some language programs spoken language will be given the primary focus. This is especially the case in beginning ESL programs where students have a strong motivation to develop speaking skills in order to participate in the second language environment. Many EFL courses also aim to give students practice in speaking for different situations. However in other programs, such as English for Academic Purposes, the focus is generally on written language because it is assumed that students should concentrate on developing skills in reading and writing academic texts, although time may also be given to preparing students to listen to lectures and present tutorial papers.

As discussed in Chapter 3, in traditional approaches to language teaching reading and writing tended to take precedence over the teaching of speaking and listening. With the introduction of communicative approaches to language teaching, however, the general focus shifted towards spoken language. The term *communicative* has often been interpreted as relating to speaking only, and in some cases this has meant that the teaching of speaking has taken precedence over the teaching of reading and writing (Hammond et al 1992).

Over recent years there has been more ethnographic and linguistic research undertaken into the uses people make of language in social contexts and this research has clearly indicated that in most social situations people use both spoken and written language to achieve their purposes. For example, when you open a new savings account at the bank you may encounter the following mixture of spoken and written texts.

Spoken	Written	Spoken	Written	Spoken	Written
Customer inquiry about types of savings accounts	Brochures outlining types of savings accounts	Explanation of procedure for opening a new account	Application form	Checking application form and asking for items of identification	Letter from bank with enclosed access card and information about its use

If students are learning language in order to use it in social situations, then it is important to take into account the linguistic and ethnographic research that clearly indicates there should be an integration of spoken and written language in most language courses as this integration of skills will prepare students to participate more effectively in social situations.

It is also important that we understand that the development of spoken language is not simply a matter of learning skills, such as pronouncing English sounds or being able to produce single utterances or phrases. Quite the contrary, the development of speaking is an ongoing and complex process of acquiring knowledge and developing skills and strategies to interact with people in social situations. From the very beginning levels of language learning students need to:

- experience various kinds of spoken texts
- develop knowledge about how social and cultural contexts affect the type of spoken language used
- learn how to participate in different spoken interactions
- expand their language resources and learn to use a range of spoken language strategies
- learn how different spoken texts are constructed
- develop greater control of the systems of vocabulary, grammar, phonology and intonation
- develop skills which will enable them to predict what will occur in a conversation
- improve their accuracy and fluency.

They will also need to develop a critical perspective on spoken language which will enable them to understand how speakers embed their values, beliefs and attitudes in their spoken language.

TASK 4.1

1 What is the balance in your language program between spoken and written language
2 When do you focus on speaking skills?

Analysing student needs

Decisions about teaching speaking will inevitably depend on the learner group and their needs in developing speaking skills. The most important starting point when deciding how to teach speaking is to gather background data about the students. This involves gathering personal data, such as age, language background and previous language learning, and information about their goals and needs and the contexts in which they will need to use English. It also involves assessing their current level of spoken language competency or proficiency.

Level of English

Assessment tools which enable the teacher to describe a stage or level of spoken language proficiency can be used initially to place students into an appropriate class. Chapter 7 provides detailed information on the purposes of assessment and assessment tools.

There is a sense in language teaching that language develops across different stages or levels. This sense of development is built into the descriptions of various course books and curricula.

When assessing speaking for initial placement teachers will probably describe the students according to:

- a continuum – from beginner to advanced with various stages of development in between (eg beginner, post beginner, low intermediate, intermediate, upper intermediate or advanced)
- levels of certification – such as the Cambridge Certificate levels or levels of certification in a curriculum framework – such as the NSW AMES Certificates I, II, III and IV in Spoken and Written English (AMES 1995)
- a rating scale – such as the Australian Second Language Proficiency Ratings (ASLPR) scale (Ingram and Wylie 1984)

Sometimes these systems can overlap, for instance a curriculum may have levels which are described in terms of stages of language development and according to a rating scale. The Certificates I, II, III and IV in Spoken and Written English are an example of this (see Figure 4.1).

Certificate I in Spoken and Written English	Certificate II in Spoken and Written English	Certificate III in Spoken and Written English	Certificate IV in Spoken and Written English
ASLPR 0 to 0+	ASLPR 1- to 1	ASLPR 1+ to 2	ASLPR 2+

Figure 4.1: Example of assessment for speaking using a combination of levels and rating scale (NSW AMES 1995)

These initial placement descriptions are meant to be only a general description. They simply enable us to make predictions about what students are likely to be able to do in speaking, and what they probably cannot do. These descriptions are likely to be tempered once the teacher gets to know the students and can undertake a more definitive analysis of their ability.

Consider the following case study:

As an initial assessment of students in a workplace course, a teacher asked a student to recount what he did on the previous weekend. He had difficulty with this task and the teacher assessed his spoken language skills as quite low.
Later in the course the teacher was teaching the students to explain problems with machinery at work. She found that this same student could do this more difficult task very well.

How would you explain this?

When to introduce authentic discourse

Student competency in spoken language will be a deciding factor in how early and in what manner authentic discourse is introduced into the language program. By authentic discourse we mean actual instances of native speakers interacting in social contexts. Although it will be more difficult for lower level students to deal with authentic discourse, it is important that they are introduced to some degree of authentic spoken texts so that they can begin to feel more confident to interact outside the classroom. The teacher can carefully control the introduction of authentic discourse into the classroom by:

- limiting the length of the discourse
- carefully preparing the students for what they will encounter in the authentic language
- carefully designing the task which the students have to undertake in relation to the authentic language.

Students' needs and goals

In deciding what spoken language to include in a program, it is valuable to investigate the students' purposes and goals for improving their speaking skills. This can be done through interviews, individual and class discussions and through class surveys. In some teaching contexts it is helpful to use a needs analysis tool such as a communication network (see Figure 4.2). The students place themselves in the middle of the network and indicate the situations in which they use or wish to use spoken language. In the example in Figure 4.2 the student is in a work-related language class and has indicated a number of situations in which he uses spoken language and has asterisked the ones in which he is having difficulty.

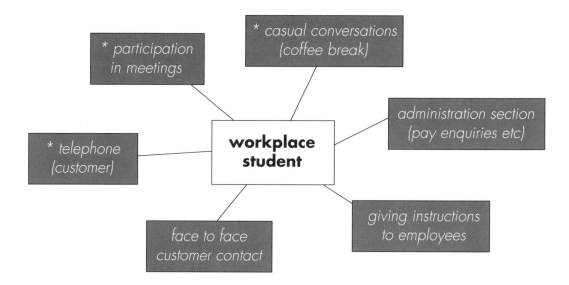

Figure 4.2: Example of a communication network

Students may have short-term goals for improving their speaking skills which they may be able to state clearly. For example, they may want to participate in casual conversations at work or perform more effectively in job interviews. They may want to be able to ask questions in a training course or they may want to be able to talk to their children's teachers. Other students may not be able to state an immediate goal but may want to improve their overall speaking skills in order to participate more effectively in a range of situations. They may want to improve their ability to use the telephone for business purposes, for example, or they may want to engage in conversations with native speakers.

Some students may simply consider that learning a language involves learning to speak and may believe that it is up to the teacher to decide what they should learn. Many recently arrived migrants who are learning the language of their adopted country do not know how to develop specific language learning goals until they have more experience of social contexts outside the classroom. In this case, the teacher could present a list of texts or topics to the students and encourage them to decide what ones they wish to cover in the course. If they cannot decide then the teacher needs to make the decision and try to explain why they have made a particular choice.

1 How have you investigated the speaking goals of your students?
2 What goals do your current students have for learning to speak English?

Considering learners' needs when programming

Speaking in social contexts

Teachers need to be aware of the spoken language demands of the social contexts beyond the classroom which their students wish to access. They must be able to analyse the highly predictable elements of texts and contexts and be able to present these explicitly to their students (see Chapter 2). Teachers should also be able to introduce unpredictable elements – which are a feature of spoken interactions outside the classroom – as their students' spoken language skills progress.

Teachers need to be aware that even the most common interactions can undergo quite rapid change. For example, in Australia, for many years we telephoned Directory Assistance to ask an employee of the telephone company for a telephone number and engaged in exchanges similar to Text 1 below (Burns, Joyce and Gollin 1996:32):

Text 1: Telephoning for directory assistance
O = operator C = caller

O:	Directory assistance
C:	Could I have the number for W Dess Glenmore Rd Paddington?
O:	Just a moment ..... That's 321 0984
C:	321
O:	0984
C:	0984
O:	Yes
C:	Thank you Bye
O:	Bye

Now that computerised telephone number databases have been introduced, although we make our request to a living, breathing telephone company employee who asks us to hold for the number, the answer we receive is from a computer. This has led to truncated exchanges like Text 2 (Burns, Joyce and Gollin 1996: 33).

Text 2 Truncated directory enquiry
O = operator   C = caller

O:	Directory assistance
C:	Could I please have the number for W Dess Glenmore Rd Paddington?
O:	Hold for the number
C:	Thanks

While technology continues to change the way we communicate, there are also other changes influencing the way we use spoken language. For example, workplaces are currently undergoing enormous changes, and employees are required to participate in a broader range of formal and informal interactions within the workplace. As a consequence the spoken language demands being placed on them are increasing: team-based work practices mean employees must be able to give opinions and explain

59

processes and procedures and they must also be able to solve problems collaboratively and negotiate with others. In addition, employees are now expected to undertake more training, and much of this training occurs off the job in formal training contexts in which they need to understand and use abstracted spoken language. Language programs which aim to develop language skills for further study or for employment need to consider these increasing and changing spoken language demands. Table 4.1 (adapted from Joyce *et al* 1995) summarises some of the increasing spoken language demands in workplaces.

Table 4.1: Increased spoken language demands in the workplace

Changes in workplace	Spoken language demands
1 Industrial relations	• summarise and explain written procedures • seek clarification of job descriptions • explain graphs, diagrams, tables
2 Government and union policies	• explain, discuss and describe occupational health and safety procedures • orally report on an accident at work
3 New technologies	• explain or describe new technology • report to group or team on new procedures • report problems and difficulties
4 Teamwork	• solve problems and negotiate solutions and outcomes • initiate and participate in team discussions • know how to challenge • know how to ask for advice • argue for and against a proposition • ask a speaker to clarify or explain a point
5 Role of the manager	• explain and discuss changes in workplace practices • explain and negotiate team membership • negotiate allocation of task • listen and discuss openly problems and issues that arise • explain section interests and needs to others
6 Role of the operator	• provide on the job instruction • understand enquiries, questions and problems experienced by the operator • summarise and explain written procedures to other operators • identify and rectify emerging problems and anticipate and predict outcomes and consequences of tasks
7 Training	• group work • lectures • activity instructions • use of questions • report on training

Speaking in the classroom

In considering students' speaking needs, we should also consider the role of spoken language in the classroom. Spoken language is central to the management of the classroom and we should be aware of the level and types of spoken language we use, as teachers, to manage the classroom. We need to spend time in programs focusing on the language of classroom management and the interpersonal uses of language within the classroom environment. If we ask students to participate in classroom activities, we need to make sure that we use spoken instructions which they can understand. We also need to familiarise students with the types of texts which we use to manage the classroom and the texts which develop classroom social interactions.

1 What do you use spoken language for in the classroom?
2 Record a segment of your next lesson and note down the ways you used spoken language in managing the classroom

Students will not all bring the same resources to the process of learning English. Some students may have had limited formal learning experiences, for example those who have come form war-torn countries and have had disrupted schooling. These students may not be aware of the uses of spoken language in the classroom and may not be prepared for the way teachers use spoken language to manage the classroom.

Some students with minimal competency in spoken language may not be able to distinguish between the spoken language of classroom management and the spoken language which teachers are trying to teach. For example, students can be confused when the teacher moves rapidly from explaining a language feature to giving instructions for a classroom activity. It is helpful, therefore, to develop ways of signalling the different types of spoken language in the classroom and use these consistently throughout a program.

Speaking outside the classroom

When making realistic judgements about how quickly students will develop spoken language, it is important to consider the opportunities they have to practise spoken language outside the classroom, and their willingness to take advantage of these opportunities. Knowing how often students are likely to engage in spoken interactions outside the classroom will influence decisions about what spoken language texts to introduce into the program. It will also influence the types of out-of-class tasks set to encourage the students to interact outside the classroom.

TASK 4.5

1 Survey your current students to find how many times each week they speak English outside the classroom.
2 Do you think this is sufficient for them to practise English in social contexts?
3 If not, how could you encourage them to increase the times they use English?

Individual and class profiles

In this section we present a number of individual student and class profiles based on an analysis of the students' speaking needs. The profiles are presented as a way of investigating the relationship between needs analysis and teaching.

Profile 1: A migrant class in a second language context

Background	• recently migrated • mixed language backgrounds of Vietnamese, Laotian, Thai and Cambodian • all male • age range from 24-40 years
Formal learning	• all literate in their first languages • first English class in new country • all learnt English at school
Language level	• beginner skills in spoken English with marked pronunciation and intonation problems • intermediate skills in written English
Access to spoken English	• limited access to English interactions outside the classroom • shop in contexts where their first languages spoken • do not venture much into English speaking contexts • listen to radio programs in their own languages • all have televisions • all have children enrolled in school
Goals	• to obtain employment – all have applied for jobs but have not been successful
Course details	20 hours per week x 20 weeks = 400 hours • 4 hours per day • government funded course

Implications for course design

In planning a course for this class you would:
• have clear aims for the overall program and class activities and communicate these to the learners
• focus the course on job seeking and preparation for workplace contexts
• aim to improve skills in:
    - listening to and speaking English in job seeking contexts

- making enquiries and seeking information in service situations
- giving relevant personal information required in job seeking contexts
- explaining Asian names and spelling them in job seeking situations
- decide on appropriate spoken and written texts in relation to job seeking and job interviews
- provide background cultural knowledge on job seeking practices within second language context.

Implications for teaching

In teaching this class you would:

- use students' higher level skills in reading and writing to support the teaching of speaking
- support texts in class with clues about the social context in which the text occurs
- use authentic texts in the classroom
- provide guided practice in developing appropriate spoken texts such as job interviews
- develop appropriate vocabulary for describing skills and experience
- focus on pronunciation and intonation
- set a range of out-of-class tasks which extend engagement with English in social contexts (eg phoning in response to advertisements).

Profile 2: A Korean hotel worker in a second language context

Background	• Korean • female • mid twenties
Formal learning	• literate in first language • first English class in new country • learnt English at school
Language level	• upper intermediate skills in written English • some pronunciation and intonation problems • intermediate skills in spoken English
Access to spoken English	• works in second language environment of 5-star hotel as waitress • deals with range of English speaking customers • uses Korean language skills when dealing with Korean guests • listens to radio programs • watches television • socialises in English-speaking contexts
Goals	• to become a tourist guide
Course details	• 1.5 hours per week • individual tuition

Implications for course design

In planning a course for this student you would:
- take into account that little face-to-face teaching time is available
- use the English speaking environment to improve listening and speaking skills
- set many out-of-class tasks which make the most of her socialising and work situations
- use TV, radio and films which student will encounter outside the classroom
- focus on pronunciation and intonation
- focus on transactional spoken language (eg service encounters)
- focus on interpersonal uses of spoken language (eg casual conversation — topics, text types (eg anecdotes)
- focus on speaking strategies.

Implications for teaching

In teaching this class you would:
- direct student in her own learning outside the classroom
- provide a mixture of prepared and authentic materials
- set regular tasks each week (eg listening to the radio)
- give student some strategies for self-monitoring and self assessment
- encourage student to give feedback in interactions
- use student feedback on out-of-class tasks to discuss other learning strategies.

Profile 3: A high school class in a foreign language context

Background	• high school class • mixed group – up to 40 students • junior high school group – Grade 8
Formal learning	• literate in first language • English classes begin in first year of junior secondary Grade 7
Language level	• beginner level
Access to spoken English	• limited access to native speakers of English • limited opportunity to watch English speaking movies or listen to English speaking radio programs
Goals	• to pass subject in high school curriculum • to use English in the longer term in employment
Tuition details	• prescribed textbook based on structural approach • prescribed curriculum framework • 4 hours per week • opportunity to work with first language teacher in team-teaching situation

Implications for course design

In planning a course for this student you would need to:

- take into account the limited opportunities to engage with native speakers of English
- encourage students to see language as a means of communication
- integrate spoken language into a set curriculum framework
- work within textbook framework
- make use of English-speaking media
- focus on pronunciation and intonation
- set up small-group, spoken-language sessions with cooperation of first language teacher.

Implications for teaching

In teaching this class you would:

- set up group and pair work activities
- gradually introduce some authentic spoken discourse texts
- set regular tasks each week to listen to English-speaking radio or movies
- align spoken language to topics or structures covered within textbook and class
- invite native speakers to the classroom if possible
- work on increasing student confidence and willingness to use English.

Profile 4: An engineer working in a second language context

Background	• 36 years old • working in large company as an engineer
Formal learning	• tertiary education • professional qualifications gained in home country • studied English from senior high school to university
Language level	• upper intermediate spoken • advanced written skills
Access to spoken English	• works in second language environment • lives in second language environment with children enrolled in schools • wife also works as a professional
Goals	• to improve ability to put forward and support personal ideas • to improve ability to engage in casual conversation
Tuition details	• 4 hours per week for 10 weeks • workplace course

Implications for course design

In planning a course for this student you would:
- focus on meeting skills
- improve skills in opinion giving in a formal context
- explore cultural and social purpose of opinion giving in professional contexts
- focus on casual conversation topics, texts and strategies.

Implications for teaching

In teaching this student you would:
- use authentic tapes of native speakers giving opinions
- use authentic tapes of workplace meetings
- explicitly teach generic structures of spoken texts
- explicitly discuss and model discourse strategies.

 Think about the last course you taught or the one you are teaching now and consider what information about the students you used to plan your course and how this information influenced your teaching.

REVIEW

In this chapter we have considered aspects of speaking in language programs. We have discussed the need to analyse:
- student competence
- student goals and needs
- students' previous formal learning experiences
- student participation in spoken English interactions outside the classroom.

The importance of understanding the spoken language demands of workplaces and other social contexts beyond the classroom was also discussed.

A number of analyses of the needs of individual students and classes were presented in order to investigate the relationship between needs analysis, course design and teaching.

References

Burns, A., H. Joyce and S. Gollin 1996. I *see what you mean*. Sydney: NCELTR.

Certificates I, II, III & IV in Spoken and Written English. 1995. Sydney: NSW AMES.

Hammond, J., A. Burns, H. Joyce, D. Brosnan, L. Gerot. 1992. English for social purposes. Sydney: NCELTR.

Hood, S. and H. Joyce. 1995. Reading in the adult ESL curriculum and classroom. *Prospect* 10.2: 52-64.

Ingram, D. and E. Wylie. 1982. *Australian Second Language Proficiency Ratings (ASLPR)*. Canberra: AGPS.

Joyce, H., C. Nesbitt, H. Scheeres, D. Slade and N. Solomon. 1995. *Team work – Effective communication in the restructured workplace: A training program*. Melbourne. National Food Industry Training Council.

Further reading

Brindley, G. 1989. The role of needs analysis in adult ESL programme design. In R.K. Johnson. *The second language curriculum*. Cambridge: Cambridge Universtiy Press.

Cornish, S. 1992. *Community access: Curriculum guidelines*. Sydney: NSW AMES.

Er, E. 1994. *A language syllabus for jobseekers*. Sydney: NSW AMES.

Syllabus design. No 25.August 1994. *Interchange, Journal of the NSW Adult Migrant English Service*.

Johnson, R.K. *The second language curriculum*. Cambridge: Cambridge University Press.

Nunan, D. and J. Burton (eds). 1989. National curriculum project frameworks 1–8. Sydney: NCELTR.

Nunan, D. 1988. *Language teaching course design: Trends and issues*. Sydney: NCELTR.

Nunan, D. 1988. *The learner-centred curriculum*. Cambridge: Cambridge University Press.

Richards, J. C. 1990. *The language teaching matrix*. Cambridge: Cambridge University Press.

FIVE

PLANNING FOR SPEAKING IN THE LANGUAGE PROGRAM

- How do you decide what spoken language to teach?
- How do you integrate spoken language into your course design?
- How do you decide on the sequencing of the content?

Deciding on the spoken language focus of a course

The extent to which a teacher makes decisions about what they teach and how they teach depends on the teaching context. In some contexts the syllabus is pre-determined and the day-to-day content is outlined in a syllabus document or in a course book which must be followed. Sometimes even methodology is specified. In these types of contexts teachers have no decision-making role in relation to content. In other contexts, however, the teacher is solely responsible for the development of the teaching program. This is usually in one-off courses where the students will not progress through different class levels in an institution. Courses in these contexts are usually based on the goals and needs of the students.

A teaching situation which lies mid-way between these two extremes is one in which the teacher works within a broad curriculum framework. Such curricula specify broad learning outcomes at different stages of language development, but the teacher is responsible for determining the texts and contexts through which the outcomes will be achieved. For example, at a particular level a curriculum may specify that students need to be able to participate in a complex spoken interaction but the teacher has to decide how to contextualise this outcome. For instance, if teaching in a workplace situation, a teacher could choose the context of a workplace meeting and use a text that involves students in presenting a workplace safety problem to a safety committee. However, the same curriculum outcome could be met in a community oriented course by choosing a social context in which students practise making a complaint to a local service provider, such as the telephone company.

In teaching contexts which require choices about what and how to teach, some of the questions which will need to be addressed are:

- Should I use a course book ?
- What spoken texts should I incorporate into the program?
- What am I aiming to achieve in this program?
- What knowledge do my students need to have?
- What speaking skills and strategies do they need to develop?
- What objectives should I set?
- What activities should I develop?
- Where will I start and how should I sequence my program?

Decisions about what spoken language to teach will inevitably depend on:

- the learner group
- the focus of the course
- the length and intensity of the course.

We have already discussed the gathering of background information on students in Chapter 4. Briefly, in order to make informed choices about spoken language teaching, information is needed about students'

- educational background – this will give some indication of their familiarity with formal learning situations and their expected rate of learning
- social circumstances – this will indicate how much they engage with the second language outside the classroom and whether they are likely to be able to undertake study at home
- needs and goals in studying language – this will help to determine the overall content of the course
- level of spoken language (discussed in more detail in Chapter 7).

The focus of the course, that is the purpose for running the course, will also play a part in determining what spoken language to include. There are two basic types of courses: those which have a pre-determined focus and content and those where content is not pre-determined

Courses which have a pre-determined focus and content tend to occur at higher levels of language learning or where students have a clear goal for learning language. Students enrol because they identify the course as directly meeting their needs. The content is largely determined by the focus of the course and the teacher's role is to refine the content and to decide how to teach it. Many English for Specific Purpose and workplace courses fall into this category.

Courses where content is not pre-determined tend to occur when students are at lower levels of language learning and need a more general focus, or when students have not been able to determine their goals for language learning. It is simply not possible to teach everything and so the teacher's role is to determine the focus of the course through processes of investigation and negotiation with students. The goals and interests of the students may be very diverse and teachers must find the common ground based on their professional judgment and the language requirements of the world outside the classroom.

It is important also to consider, when designing courses, how much time is available. We are often overwhelmed by the wide range of needs which the students articulate and we may try to achieve too much, especially when working with lower level students. However it is much better to stand back and make a considered decision about how much is actually achievable in the time available.

Designing the language program

A course outline gives direction to the course; it ensures that all relevant aspects of the students' needs and background have been taken into account and ensures appropriate weighting to various aspects of the program. Given that all courses are finite, a course outline ensures that the most important aspects of language development for the particular target group are covered.

A course outline also provides students with information about what the teacher has planned and why particular decisions have been made about what they will learn. It is particularly important for lower level students to have a sense of direction. This does not mean that teachers cannot divert from their plan of action if the need arises, but the course outline is an important area of shared knowledge between students and teacher. There are, in fact, many factors which may lead a class away from the course plan and it is important that teachers allow for flexibility in order to respond to the needs of students which arise during course delivery.

Stages in overall program design

The development of a language course follows a number of stages depending on the starting point that has been chosen. In this section the basic stages are broadly outlined. Tables 5.1 and 5.2 at the end of this chapter describe in more detail the steps involved in designing language programs from different starting points and present examples from actual programs.

Stage 1: Decide on a starting point

The staring point indicates broad categories of content. Two popular approaches to planning the overall content and program structure are:
- starting with topics
- starting with texts.

Starting with topics

A topic approach to content is widely accepted in all areas of education, and in language teaching it is often adopted where the needs of students or the focus of a course are quite broad, for instance in a course with a community access focus. Topics provide a focus for selecting materials, tasks and teaching resources and can be used to link a range of different speaking activities by providing a common thread. By staying within one topic over a period of time, key vocabulary can be recycled through different texts and activities, thus reducing the need for students to be constantly learning new language.

Topics may arise from the needs students have identified for language learning. For example, if students state the need to participate more effectively in the broader community, then appropriate topics might be: public transport, health, your child's school, shopping and so on. Even in courses with a predetermined focus, topics for language learning can be used. For example, in a further study course where students are preparing to study in a formal tertiary context topics may be used to provide appropriate fields for language study. Topics chosen might include the environment, drugs in society or technology in a changing world. Once the topics have been chosen, then the teacher needs to decide on the texts which will be included within the topic area. The steps involved in planning a topic-based program are detailed in Table 5.1.

If you were teaching a group of students who were interested in current affairs as a vehicle for language learning what topics would you set?

Starting with texts

Another approach to planning courses is to start with the texts which are identified for a specific context or which have been identified by the students. This approach is often used when an overall context for language learning has been defined, such as in a specific workplace or a university or other further study context. Units of work are then developed in relation to the texts. For example, the spoken texts identified for a group of engineers in a workplace were: spoken instructions to field staff, presentations of report findings at meetings and telephone negotiations with contractors. The steps involved in planning a text-based program are detailed in Table 5. 2.

What spoken texts would you choose for a language course preparing students for job seeking?

Stage 2: Develop goals or aims

Once the texts have been selected, either within broader topic areas or as separate areas of content, then goals or aims need to be developed. These are the broad statements of intent and provide a statement of purpose for language teaching and learning. It is important that the broad goals of a program are stated clearly and that students understand what the program and teacher are seeking to achieve.

In courses with a pre-determined focus and content the goals are generally stated before the program begins. Students enrol because they identify the goals as meeting their needs. An example of such aims (for a further study course) is given overleaf.

This course aims to:
- prepare students to study in a tertiary institution
- develop research skills appropriate to tertiary study
- develop writing skills appropriate to specific disciplines
- develop listening skills in order to listen to lectures
- develop appropriate speaking skills for tutorial presentations
- develop a range of study skills including time and resource management.

In courses where the content is not pre-determined it is the teacher's role to determine the goals or aims of the course through processes of investigation and negotiation with the students. For example, the aims of a community access course may be stated as follows:

This course aims to:
- provide students with cultural and social knowledge
- develop language skills which will enable students to participate effectively in a range of community contexts
- develop learning skills which will enable students to use community contexts as a resource for language learning.

Stage 3: Sequence content

A course should be a logical sequencing of language learning which integrates spoken and written language. The logic behind sequencing decisions should be shared with the students as this gives them a sense of direction and can make them feel more comfortable with the general direction of the course.

If programming is on the basis of topics then the order in which topics are presented may depend on the interests of the students or on how their needs have been prioritised. More familiar or easier topics might be presented first and then followed by topics which are less familiar or more demanding.

As most programs need to integrate spoken and written language, the language event sequence is a helpful tool for ordering spoken and written texts. (Figure 5.1 illustrates the language event sequence centred around the breakdown of a household appliance such as a washing machine.) Such sequences provide a way of presenting the learning of spoken texts in an order which reflects their occurrence and relationship to written texts outside the classroom. Using a language event sequence also highlights the way in which spoken language forms an integral part of the events that make up our daily lives and demonstrates the interrelatedness of spoken and written texts. Using language event sequences to integrate spoken texts into the language program enables students to understand what they will need to learn in order to participate in similar events in social contexts outside the classroom.

Spoken	Spoken	Spoken	Written	Written	Written
Telephone call to washing machine repair service to book a time	Service call and face-to-face explanation of problem	Statement of cost and explanation of repairs carried out	Invoice for repairs	Payment by: • cash • cheque, or • credit card	Receipt

Figure 5.1: Language event sequence centred around the breakdown of a household appliance

Stage 4: Developing units of work and setting objectives

After deciding on the content and the overall sequence for the program, the specific focus for each teaching unit has to be determined and the units designed. One way to ensure that spoken language is given appropriate weighting in the teaching unit is to make the focus of the unit a spoken text, a specific speaking skill or strategy, a specific phonological feature or a grammatical structure used in spoken language.

The objectives for a teaching unit relate back to the overall goals of the program. They describe what knowledge or skills the students are expected to develop. It is important to share these objectives at the beginning of a teaching unit with your students, if this is possible. Like sharing the goals, sharing the objectives gives the students a sense of direction and a sense of having some control over the learning process. Some of the types of objectives that can be set in relation to speaking are listed below. The divisions between these objectives are not clear cut but, it is useful to think about different types of objectives when you are planning a program.

Objectives related to knowledge

These objectives aim to develop knowledge about:
- the role of spoken language in the broader culture
- social situations and how they predict spoken language
- a topic area in order to develop vocabulary in preparation for speaking
- appropriate conversational topics
- turn types in conversation
- speaker roles in conversation
- non-verbal conventions
- how spoken texts are organised to achieve particular social purposes
- how grammar works in spoken language to make certain kinds of meanings

- the phonological systems of English
- intonation and stress patterns
- the role of backchannelling and feedback in conversation.

Objectives related to skills
These objectives aim to develop skills such as:
- turn taking
- giving feedback and backchannelling
- maintaining conversations
- initiating conversations
- closing interactions appropriately
- guessing the meaning of unfamiliar words
- seeking clarification
- asking for repetition
- structuring spoken information
- giving spoken instructions
- developing spoken texts such as anecdotes
- using appropriate vocabulary
- using appropriate intonation and stress patterns.

TASK 5.3

A number of teaching activities are described below. What do you think the teachers' objectives were in designing these activities?

- Teacher A gives her students the transcript of a spoken text and as they listen to it on audio tape she asks them to mark how the speakers give feedback to one another.
- Teacher B asks his students to listen to a tape and note how many different pieces of information they hear about a topic.
- Teacher C divides her class into pairs and gives them cue cards for a roleplay. They are to role play buying a ticket at the railway station.
- Teacher D asks students to complete a survey, by interviewing other students, on where people live and how they get to class.
- Teacher E drills her students in short answer forms (eg No I don't)
- Teacher F explains to his students about the influence of people's status on spoken interactions.
- Teacher G gives her students some homework. They are to tell the class during the next lesson two ways they heard native speakers start a conversation.
- Teacher H uses the transcript of a doctor's consultation on an OHT to point out the stages of the discourse to her students.
- Teacher I practises imperative structures in preparation for teaching spoken instructions.
- Teacher J breaks the class into groups of three. Two students have to engage in a conversation and the third has to interrupt politely.
- Teacher K arranges an excursion to a museum and gives each student the task of asking museum staff a specified question.

Sample program and teaching unit designs

Table 5.1 details the steps involved in using a topic approach to program design and focuses on the topic of Public Transport from a Community Access course. In Step 3 a language event sequence is used to identify the specific texts. The spoken language texts and activities are highlighted in bold.

Table 5.1: Designing a course from topics (Adapted from Burns, Joyce and Gollin 1996: 75–6)

Step	Discussion and examples
1 Identify topic	Public transport (because the course focus is community access and students are new arrivals in the city)
2 Develop an aim	To develop the spoken and written language skills required to make effective use of the public transport system
3 Note the language event sequence	Using public transport in the community: • reading timetables • reading transport route maps • **enquiring about schedules** • **buying a ticket face to face** • buying a ticket through a machine • **listening to transport announcements** • **enquiring about delays**
4 List the texts arising from the sequence	• Timetables • Maps • **Service encounter – enquiry about schedules** • **Service encounter – buying a ticket** • Procedural text – instructions for ticket machine • **Platform announcements** • **Service encounter – enquiry about delays**
5 Outline the sociocultural knowledge students need	To use public transport students need knowledge about: • the overall transport system in the city • ticketing procedures such as the use of ticket machines and the role of ticket inspectors • sources of transport information
6 Record or gather samples of texts	• Written texts: Gather examples of timetables, procedural texts etc • Spoken texts: You may need to: – find available recordings – prepare some semi-scripted dialogues yourself – record authentic interactions
7 Develop units of work related to the texts and develop learning objectives to be achieved	Classroom activities and tasks should be sequenced within units of work to provide students with: • explicit input • guided practice • an opportunity to perform independently
8 Develop tasks which students can undertake outside the classroom	These tasks should: • be achievable • encourage students to practise language outside the classroom • be monitored in the following lesson

Complete a table similar to Table 5.1 for a topic on health.

Table 5.2 on page 79 details the stages involved in designing a program on the basis of texts and uses an English for Academic Purposes course as an example. The spoken language texts and activities are highlighted in bold.

Complete a table similar to Table 5.2 for a 'language of job seeking' course.

This chapter outlined how we make decisions about what spoken language to teach based on:

- the learner group
- the focus of the course
- the length and intensity of the course

The stages involved in program design were also outlined. These included:

- deciding on content from:
  - a topic-based approach where the content of a course is divided into topics and then the spoken texts which students need to study are identified within the topics
  - a text-based approach where the context for language learning has been defined and the spoken texts which are necessary for effective participation in the context are identified
- developing goals or aims
- sequencing content
- developing units of work and setting objectives

The chapter concluded with two sample program designs. One was based on topics and the other was based on texts.

Table 5.2: Designing a course from texts (Adapted from Burns, Joyce and Gollin 1996: 78–80)

Step	Discussion and examples
1 Identify the overall context	University: course focus is preparing students for study at university
2 Develop an aim	To develop the spoken and written language skills required to undertake university study
3 Note the language event sequence within the context	These could include: • **enrolling at university** • **discussing course selection** • **attending lectures** • **attending tutorials** • **using the library** • reading reference books • writing essays • writing reports • undertaking examinations • **participating in casual conversations**
4 List the texts arising from the sequence	These could include: • enrolment forms • **service encounter – selecting courses** • **lectures** • **tutorial discussions** • **service encounter – library enquiry** • Range of possible written texts, for example: – discipline-specific essays – discipline-specific reports • Range of possible reading texts, for example: – discipline-specific journal articles – discipline-specific books – library catalogues – lecture notes • examination papers • **genres within casual conversation (eg anecdote)**
5 Outline the sociocultural knowledge students need	Students need knowledge about: • academic institutions • academic procedures and expectations • the role of the student
6 Record or gather samples of texts	• Written texts: Gather examples of essays, catalogues, journals etc • Spoken texts: You may need to: – find available recordings – prepare some semi-scripted dialogues yourself – record authentic interactions
7 Develop units of work related to the texts and develop learning objectives to be achieved	Classroom tasks should be sequenced within units of work to provide students with: • explicit input • guided practice • an opportunity to perform independently

References

Burns, A., H. Joyce and S. Gollin. 1996. *I see what you mean. Using spoken discourse in the classroom: A handbook for teachers.* Sydney: NCELTR.

Further reading

Brown, J.D. 1995. *The elements of language curriculum.* Boston, Mass: Heinle and Heinle.

Brumfit, C. 1986. *Communicative methodology in language teaching.* Cambridge: Cambridge University Press.

Cornish, S. 1992. *Community access : Curriculum guidelines.* Sydney: NSW AMES.

Dubin, F. and E. Olshtain. 1986. *Course design.* New York: Cambridge University Press.

Hammond, J., A. Burns, H. Joyce, D. Brosnan and L. Gerot. 1992. *English for social purposes.* Sydney: NCELTR.

Joyce, H. 1992. *Workplace texts.* Sydney: NSW AMES.

Nunan, D. 1988. *Syllabus design.* Oxford: Oxford University Press.

Nunan, D. 1987. *The teacher as curriculum developer.* Sydney: NCELTR.

Widdowson, H. G. 1990. *Aspects of language teaching.* Oxford: Oxford University Press.

Yalden, J. 1987. *Principles of course design for language teaching.* Cambridge: Cambridge University Press.

SIX

SPEAKING ACTIVITIES IN THE CLASSROOM

Think of a lesson or unit of work which you have taught recently:

- What kinds of spoken texts did you use and why did you select them?
- Did you use any authentic recordings of native speakers?
- What kind of speaking activities did you use and why did you select them?

> We…have long had the question of how people use language uppermost in our minds when we design teaching materials, or when we engage learners in exercises and activities aimed at making them proficient users of their target language, or when we evaluate a piece of commercially published material before deciding to use it. (McCarthy 1991: 1)

After analysing the needs and goals of the students, and planning the overall aims and direction of a language program, decisions need to be made about what will be done in the classroom. The teacher has to design teaching-learning sequences which will develop the students' ability to use spoken language. These sequences are based on the selected spoken texts and the classroom activities and must allow for the introduction, practice, recycling and extension of skills and knowledge. The teacher needs to decide:

- what spoken texts they will present to the students
- what activities they will use or design
- what roles the teacher and the students will play in the teaching-learning processes of the classroom.

Selecting spoken texts for the classroom

When teaching spoken language, teachers can present three forms of spoken texts to their students:

- scripted texts, which are generally found in course books
- authentic texts, which are recordings of native speakers in contexts outside the classroom
- semi-scripted materials.

These materials are all appropriate in the classroom, but the teacher must be aware that scripted and semi-scripted dialogues will not necessarily prepare students to speak to native speakers outside the classroom. If materials are intended to prepare students to use language in social contexts, then they must be based on authentic spoken language.

Scripted dialogues

In language teaching, speaking has often been taught through the use of dialogues. These are usually invented or scripted by a textbook writer and are based on intuitions or assumptions about what people say when they speak. They represent an idealised version of how speakers interact in different situational contexts, but the kind of language presented is usually very different from real samples of natural speech. This is because idealised versions of oral language have usually been derived from grammars which are based on written rather than spoken language.

Read the following two texts and answer the questions below:

1 Which of these texts is scripted?
2 What aspects of the language suggest this?
3 Which of these texts is not scripted?
4 What aspects of the language suggest this?

Text 1

S1: Good morning, er, Glebe Osteopathic Centre

S2: Oh, hi, I was wondering if I could make an appointment to see Karen.

S1: Karen, yep … er … when did you want to make that for?

S2: Is there any chance of seeing her today?

S1: Er, no … she's booked out now I'm sorry.

S2: Oh, um … and when's she working next?

S1: Um, oh, well Monday.

S2: OK, well I'd better make it Monday.

S1: OK. In the morning or afternoon?

S2: Uuuum … in the afternoon, any time after, say half past three?

S1: OK, um, have you been here before?

S2: Yeah, yeah.

S1: Four o'clock?

S2: Um, yeah I can get there by four.

S1: OK, what's your name?

S2: Sarah Martin

S1: Um, that's er four o'clock on Monday the eleventh with Karen.

S2: Great. Thanks very much.

S1: [Yeah, bye

S2: [Bye.

Text 2
Making an appointment with the doctor

S1: Good morning. Can I make an appointment with Dr Edwards?

S2: What is your name please?

S1: My name is Perry Morris.

S2: Are you a new patient?

S1: Yes, I am. I haven't been to Dr Edwards's surgery before.

S2: Can you come in to see the doctor on Wednesday at 4.30?

S1: Yes, I can. Thank you.

S2 All right then. Good bye.

S1: Goodbye.

It is not difficult to identify that Text 2 is a scripted dialogue. The more obvious features of this example are:

- The speakers tend to speak in fully formed sentences (*What is your name, please? Can you come in to see the doctor on Wednesday at 4.30? I haven't been to Dr Edwards's surgery before.*)
- Each speaker does about the same amount of talking.
- Each speaker takes distinct turns with no overlapping.
- There are no hesitations , such as *er* or *um* or feedback devices such as *OK*.
- The speakers use formal and standard language forms.

Apply the characteristics of Text 2, listed above, to the unscripted Text 1. What differences does this reveal?

Scripted texts are usually found transcribed in course books or teacher resources and often include an audio recording of the scripted dialogues. Consider Text 3, which is an example of a scripted dialogue focusing on asking and giving directions.

Text 3 (Burns, Joyce and Gollin 1996: 44)

A Excuse me. How do I get to the North East Shopping Centre?

B Take a number 9 bus to Westmore Street. When you reach Westmore Street, transfer to the number 34 bus at the corner of Walton Road. This bus will take you to the North East Shopping Centre.

A How will I know when I have arrived at Westmore Street?

B The bus driver will let you know if you ask him.

A Thank you. How much will it cost?

B It will cost about $3.50 altogether. You will need to have the exact money as the driver cannot give you any change.

A I see. Thank you very much. Goodbye.

Characteristics of scripted dialogues

Scripted dialogues are much easier for students to deal with, especially at lower levels of language development. However, it is important to be clear about the model of spoken language they present. Scripted texts tend to:

- be based on the writers' intuitions or assumptions about what occurs in spoken interactions
- represent spoken exchanges as neat, fully formed, predictable and unproblematic
- be based on the grammar of written English
- omit the essential grammatical features and the typical discourse strategies which native speakers use
- be based on standard pronunciation with language enunciated with precision
- repeat particular structures or functions with unnatural frequency

- present utterances as complete sentences which are short and well-formed
- show distinct turn-taking patterns where one speaker waits until the other has finished
- give speakers equal turns which slows speech down
- ignore the backchannelling strategies (eg *uhuh, ahah*) and the discourse markers (eg *right, OK*) of authentic speech
- be biased towards standard forms and structures with no swearing, slang or idioms
- restrict vocabulary to one topic of discourse
- name the things in the context.

Look at a scripted dialogue which you have used in class. Analyse it in the light of the characteristics outlined above.

Scripted dialogues can be useful, especially at the beginning stages of language learning. However, as students progress they need to be introduced to spoken interactions which reflect actual dialogues between native speakers. Spoken language has its own characteristics and we need to be able to discuss these with learners. Introducing learners to real as well as scripted samples of spoken language may help them to understand and prepare for unpredictable speaking situations outside the language classroom.

Authentic spoken texts

Many teachers try to create 'authentic' situations inside the language classroom which reflect the uses of spoken language in social situations but, in reality, the language students encounter outside the classroom is often much more challenging than the language they have been presented with in class.

If the overall aim of language programs is to prepare students to use spoken language effectively in social situations, then teachers need to present students with authentic spoken texts in the classroom. This may include the use of recordings and transcripts of authentic discourse. Teachers need to know how authentic texts differ from scripted and semi-scripted texts and how to use this knowledge to assist second language learners to develop speaking skills.

Text 4 (Burns, Joyce and Gollin 1996: 46–7)
[signifies overlapping speech
… signifies a pause

A   Um … give me an idea how I get to your place … I don't … 'cos, I don't, um, …   know it too well round there. I'll, uh … probably be coming by bus …
[so

B   [Right, well, going towards French Street, stay on the bus for, oh … about…the trip takes about twenty minutes by bus

A	Right
B	Now, you go…the bus will go out along St Katherine's Road well, you…[just keep on the bus..
A	[Mm … hm …
B	And it'll cross over Peters Road which is fairly [major…
A	[Yeah … I know Peters
B	… Hm … now, you watch out for Minter Street. It's about … oooh, fifteen minutes by bus from the corner of Peters. [Maybe …
A	[Right…uh
B	… a bit longer, maybe twenty depending on the traffic. Um, now get off at the … um, South Weston post office, which I think is two stops … two stops past Minter Street.
A	Right … that's fine …

Characteristics of unscripted dialogues

Consider Text 4 – an unscripted dialogue which, like Text 3, focuses on asking and giving directions. It illustrates many of the typical features of authentic spoken discourse, including:

- fragmented utterances which are difficult to set out as sentences
- utterances which vary greatly in length
- varied grammatical structures, some of which are incomplete
- overlappings and interruptions rather than distinct turns
- relatively frequent hesitations and backchannelling
- informal and idiomatic language
- reference to shared knowledge and understandings of locations and processes
- implied context.

As can be seen by comparing Texts 3 and 4, if students are restricted to scripted dialogues they will develop an unrealistic view of the features of spoken language and will not be prepared for their role as participants in spoken interactions in social contexts. For students to be able participate in spoken interactions outside the classroom, the teacher will need to introduce authentic discourse gradually into the classroom. Authentic spoken texts are more difficult for students to deal with and how and when students are introduced to authentic discourse will depend on their level of language and their goals.

The introduction of authentic spoken language is possible at lower levels of language development if the tasks designed around the authentic language are carefully controlled by the teacher. For example, beginning students could be asked to listen to a short fragment of authentic spoken language to identify the number of speakers and whether they are male or female. They could also practise features of authentic discourse such as contracted verb forms. Intermediate students could be asked to identify the stages of a particular spoken genre after they have been introduced to the stages in another text.

Recordings and transcriptions of authentic discourse can be used in a variety of ways with different groups of learners and for a number of different purposes. For example, they can be used to analyse different aspects and features of spoken interaction, from overall text structure to specific discourse features and strategies. They can also be used to provide learners with the opportunity to listen to native speakers as opposed to invented models of spoken discourse.

Look at an authentic dialogue that you are likely to use in class. Analyse it for the characteristics of unscripted dialogues outlined above.

Using transcripts of authentic spoken language

One advantage of using transcriptions, especially of authentic speech, is that spoken discourse can be treated as a finished product and students have a greater opportunity to analyse features of the interaction such as:

- the style of interaction
- the results of the interaction
- the relationship of the interactants
- the purpose of the interaction and whether it was achieved
- the development of the interaction
- the strategies adopted by the interactants
- the turn taking and turn type patterns
- the sociocultural values which informed the interaction.

When and how transcripts are used in the classroom will depend on the students and what the teacher is trying to achieve. The two main questions to consider when introducing transcripts to students are:

- Is the transcript too difficult?
- Do the students have sufficient literacy skills to deal with spoken language which is written down?

Look at the transcription of the spoken interaction in Text 4 and consider whether you would use this with your students. If you would, how would you use it? If you wouldn't use it, why not?

Semi-scripted texts

Scripted spoken texts generally present learners with unrealistic models of spoken interactions, and authentic texts are difficult to gather and present to students. In response to this problem, some teachers and material developers have opted for a third type of text – the semi-scripted interaction. These are texts

which are created by asking two or more people to perform a particular spoken language interaction which is recorded as they improvise. In order to produce a semi-scripted exchange you must:

- set the context
- identify a purpose for the interaction
- identify aspects of authentic discourse which should be included (eg backchannelling, idiomatic phrases etc).

These texts are a good transition between scripted and authentic texts because they introduce students to the features of authentic speech in a controlled way.

TASK 6.6

Consider a topic or a text you are currently teaching and organise to record a semi-scripted dialogue which you can use in class.

Methodology in teaching spoken language

> Methodology is an attempt both to understand and to intervene in the process of language learning. (Brumfit 1984: 23)

While most language programs recognise that language learning is a gradual process, the methodologies which have been put forward for the teaching of speaking have varied over the years (see Chapter 3).

Methodologies based on communicative approaches to teaching speaking tend to focus on spoken language *use* rather than the *form* of the language. This has meant that in the classroom the teacher has been encouraged to focus on activities which will get students speaking and little attention has been paid to providing them with the means to interact. As a result, there was often little guidance given to teachers on how to integrate a focus on the form of spoken language.

More recently, however, there has been growing interest in methodological approaches which integrate a focus on using language with a focus on form. People developing broader approaches to language teaching have been concerned to help learners understand how the form of the language allows people to do things with language in social contexts. This means that the teaching of speaking is returning to an explicit teaching of the form of language and aligning this to using the language.

A suggested methodological framework

Teachers usually draw from a range of methodological approaches in their choice of activities and tasks for the classroom. However, it is important that they make their choices within a systematic overall framework for designing lessons and lesson segments, rather than by an ad hoc selection of activity types. Having an overall framework is also useful in communicating methodological decisions to students who can sometimes be left floundering when they cannot see the teacher's rationale behind the sequencing of activities – it is important that teaching is not a game for students of guess what's in the teacher's mind.

Generally student access to formal learning is limited and therefore it is important to adopt a methodology which:

- is systematic
- can be explained to the students
- clearly identifies teacher and student roles in the classroom
- develops student independence in using spoken language
- recycles activity types so that students can concentrate on language rather than on learning to deal with constantly changing activity types.

A broad framework for planning units of work and teaching sequences is outlined in Figure 6.1. The framework is based on the notion of *scaffolding*, which involves providing systematic support for students in the learning process. The term *scaffold* was first used by Bruner (1983) and derives from the work of the Russian psychologist Vygotsky who argued that learning occurs in social situations and that learners cannot be given immediate and full responsibility for the achievement of tasks but must share this responsibility with their teachers. As a learner's competence improves, the teacher decreases the amount of support provided and learners are expected to take increasing responsibility for performance.

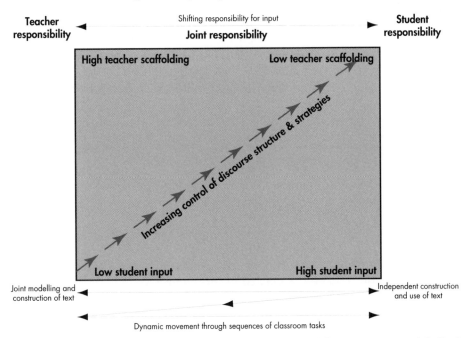

Figure 6.1: Scaffolding spoken language development (adapted from Pearson and Gallagher 1983: 344)

The notion of scaffolding is a useful one for teaching speaking as handing over full responsibility for spoken language performance to students at early stages of learning is problematic. Students may not yet have developed the skills, the vocabulary or the grammatical structures required to participate in spoken interactions. The teacher's role is to:

- provide explicit support
- provide guided practice
- think about when it is appropriate to withdraw this support as the students gradually become more able to complete tasks independently.

High teacher scaffolding occurs when spoken texts or tasks are new to the students. At beginning stages of spoken language development students are dependent on the teacher for input and explicit instruction in relation to:

- cultural, social and contextual information associated with spoken texts
- models of spoken language
- aspects of spoken language such as the structure of spoken texts, discourse strategies, vocabulary and grammar
- explanation and modelling of classroom tasks.

As student competence in speaking increases, the teacher can reduce the amount of direct modelling and guidance and the students can take a more independent role in the performance of tasks. At this stage the teacher focuses less on instruction and modelling and adopts different teaching strategies, such as:

- acting as a coach or facilitator for classroom activities
- monitoring student performance
- encouraging students to communicate and provide feedback to each other
- providing corrective feedback on task performance.

TASK 6.7

Consider the activities which the following teachers have designed for their students. Do they involve high or low teacher scaffolding?

- Teacher A asks her students to talk about their weekend using formulaic expressions which were taught previously.
- Teacher B gives her students a grammar exercise on present tense to complete at home.
- Teacher C sets up a roleplay, gives each group a tape recorder to record the roleplay and leaves the room.
- Teacher D asks students to watch a video of a casual conversation and to note the way turns are managed.
- Teacher E teaches English in a workplace. She tells the students they must speak to their supervisor about their current work. She has talked this over with the supervisors and has given them a criteria checklist for evaluating student performance.

- Teacher F puts two texts on the same topic on an OHT – one is spoken and one is written. – and analyses the differences between the two.
- Teacher G gives her students the transcript of a spoken text and as they listen to it on audio tape she asks them to mark how the speakers give feedback to one another.
- Teacher H gives students practice in linguistic structures for hypothesising (eg What if ...)
- Teacher I asks students to note the topics of conversation which occur at coffee break.

Shifting responsibility in the classroom

The notion of scaffolding leads to the idea of shifting responsibility within the classroom. That is to say, that in some phases of a lesson teachers will have the main responsibility for what is happening in the classroom, at other times they will share this responsibility with the learners, and at other times the responsibility may lie wholly with the students. This idea of shifting responsibility is depicted in Figure 6.2.

Teacher responsibility	Shared responsibility	Student responsibility
teacher centred	focus shifts continually from teacher to students	students work independently or in groups to produce language

Figure 6.2: Shifting responsibility in the classroom

As the arrow indicates, the movement from one phase to another is not necessarily in one direction. It is possible to move backwards and forwards between any of the phases according to what the teacher is trying to achieve in a lesson, and the overall cycle is likely to be repeated a number of times during a whole language teaching program.

The phases of *teacher responsibility* in a teaching sequence involve explicit input from the teacher and could involve the teacher in:

- providing information about sociocultural practices
- leading discussion
- making comparisons between L1 and L2 cultural practices
- explaining aspects of model texts to students (eg overall structure, strategies, vocabulary, grammar)
- demonstrating how to undertake classroom activities.

Meanwhile, students are participating in these phases through discussion or responses to the teacher's questions.

In phases of *shared responsibility* students will be undertaking activities which provide them with practice in aspects of spoken language. As the students work on activities, the teacher continually assesses their performance. It is in this phase of a lesson that the teacher decides whether aspects of language need to be revised, or practice extended.

When *students take responsibility* for the independent performance of tasks, they should feel that it is appropriate to give feedback to each other and that the teacher can take a back seat role.

Consider the following classroom activities. Who has the responsibility for performance or is it shared?

1   A student is delivering a short presentation to the class on education in her home country.
2   Students are sequencing a dialogue which has been typed out and then cut into pieces.
3   Students are watching a video designed to set the context for a unit of work on transport, and noting down vocabulary.
4   Students are taking turns at role playing a job interview with the teacher as the personnel officer.
5   Students are explaining how to use a vending machine to a native speaker as an assessment task.
6   Students listen as the teacher explains the feedback strategies in a transcript of authentic speech
7   Students are required to engage in conversation with native speaker visitors to the classroom.

Activity types in teaching speaking

If students are to learn about the form of spoken language as well as to gain practise in using spoken language, then teachers need to provide activities for teaching speaking which focus on both these aspects. There are a variety of sources from which to gather speaking activities. Many course books and teacher resources provide speaking activities of various kinds which can be used as they are or which can be adapted; teachers can also design their own activities to meet the particular needs of their learners. Whatever the source, the criteria for choosing particular activities is always the same – that they help students develop skills and knowledge in using spoken language

The sequence in which activities are presented is also important. In the previous section we discussed a methodological framework based on the concept of scaffolding, which is a way of systematically sequencing activities which move students towards independence. Using this framework we can group activities into five categories:
• preparation activities
• activities which focus on language awareness and skills
• activities which focus on discourse awareness and skills
• interaction activities
• extension activities.

Before we present sample activities for each of these categories, it is important to note the following points:

- Although the activities are presented in categories, many of them are relevant across categories.
- Categories of activities are not necessarily presented to students in the order listed above. Over a unit of work or a teaching sequence it is likely that the five categories will be drawn upon at different times; in fact, some teachers may start with an interaction activity, such as asking students to participate in a role play, in order to see what preparation activities need to be undertaken and what language and discourse awareness the students need to develop.
- The activities have not been categorised according to student level and most can be modified for different language levels.
- Sample activities are centred around developing language skills related to a service encounter at the post office. This is done in order to give a specific focus to the activities, but they can easily be adapted to other spoken texts.

We would also like to stress that it is not only important that the teacher is clear about the purpose of the activities when choosing, modifying or designing them, but it is also important that the students, where possible, also understand the aim of activities before taking part in an activity. This will help them to develop awareness of the learning process and give them a sense of where the lesson is going. It also assists learners to take responsibility for their own learning.

Can you think of another way to categorise speaking activities?

Preparation activities

Preparation activities help students to understand the type of spoken interaction they will be producing and the context for that interaction. These preparation activities need to draw on student experience, elicit language, develop motivation and encourage students to participate in spoken exchanges. They make speaking easier for students by preparing them for what they have to say and helping them to understand how they should participate in a spoken interaction.

The amount of time spent on preparation activities will depend on a number of factors:

- the level of the students
- the class profile ie is the class disparate in terms of spoken language proficiency, goals and experience
- class size
- the type of interaction
- the goals of the program

- whether the students have encountered this type of interaction before
- the difficulty of the spoken text which will depend on factors such as:
  – the number of interactants
  – the type of interaction (ie transactional or interactional)
  – the predictability of the discourse
  – the purpose of the interaction
  – the familiarity of the context
  – the role the student has to play in the interaction
  – the content being discussed.

Examples from a service encounter

To prepare students to participate in a service encounter at the local post-office, the following preparation activities could be used:

- Show a picture of a post office and ask the students to identify items of vocabulary.
- Discuss what students use the post office for. Often discussion will reveal that students do not have relevant knowledge or language for the interaction.
- Show a video of a post office encounter and ask students to listen for particular information within the interaction (eg how much postage was paid etc).
- Ask the students to listen for particular information in an audio recording of a post office service encounter (eg what is being sent, where a letter is being sent etc).
- Ask students to work in groups and categorise pictures of postal items taken from post office brochures (eg air mail envelopes, parcels, express paid envelopes etc).
- Ask students to listen to a simple short service encounter in the post office and repeat what the speakers say.
- Explain to students the role of the post office and what services it provides.
- Arrange an excursion to the local post office and give students a sheet to identify signs and products at the post office.

Think about a spoken interaction you are preparing students for. What preparation activities have you designed?

Activities which focus on language awareness and skills

In order to participate in spoken interaction students need to have the necessary language skills and the language necessary for effective communication. Their basic needs are for sufficient vocabulary and control of grammatical structures to produce spoken language.

Examples from a service encounter

The following language-focused activities could be used for a service encounter at the local post-office:

- Put the word post office on the board and brainstorm vocabulary.
- Give the students brochures from the local post office and ask them to look for specific vocabulary items.
- Ask students to match pictures of postal products and services with words.
- Ask students to listen to an audio tape and listen for questions which the participants ask (eg Do you want to send it air mail? etc).
- Drill students in making modalised requests (eg Could I send this to America please?).
- Drill students in asking questions (eg How much would it be to send this to Hong Kong?).
- Ask students to listen to an audio tape for ways customers enquire about services (eg How long would it take to go express mail?).

Activities which focus on discourse awareness and skills

To participate in spoken interactions students must also be aware of how participants build a spoken text together when they are speaking. In the simplest terms they must know how to begin a spoken interaction, how to maintain it and how to end it. They must also realise that there are rules and strategies which govern the way discourse is developed.

Examples from a service encounter

Discourse-focused activities for a service encounter at the local post-office could include the following:

- Ask the students to listen to audio tapes of service encounters in different contexts and note how people start the encounters.
- Ask students to listen to service encounters in local shops and note how people end them.
- Ask students to listen to a recording of a post office service encounter and to note how turn taking is controlled.
- Show students the transcript of an authentic post office service encounter on an OHT and mark and explain the stages of the discourse.
- Give students a transcript of a service encounter in a post office and ask them to mark the stages.
- Use a recording and transcript and explain the question/answer pairs to students.
- Give the students a skeleton dialogue and ask them to complete the interaction in pairs.

- Ask students to practise different ways of beginning and ending post office service encounters.
- Ask students to work in pairs and practise question-answer or offer-acceptance adjacency pairs.

Interaction activities

Essentially, all the categories of activities outlined so far aim to prepare students for spoken interactions in specific contexts. It is important that students have the opportunity to practise these spoken interactions inside the classroom and it is particularly helpful to students if they can also undertake these outside the classroom.

Examples from a service encounter

Interaction activities for a post office service encounter could include the following:
- Ask students to explain different postal services to the class.
- Ask each student to gather information on a particular postal service. Students then complete a questionnaire on postal services by asking each other questions.
- Ask students to work in pairs. Give Student 1 the postal rates for overseas mail and give Student 2 a worksheet with a number of items which have to be sent overseas. Student 2 must request the service and Student 1 must provide the information.
- Ask students to undertake a roleplay of a post office service encounter with cue cards given to pairs of students.
- Ask pairs of students to role play a service encounter in a post office and record the discourse. Transcribe parts of their tapes onto OHTs. Discuss the performances with the class as a whole.
- Give students a one-sided post office service encounter and ask them to complete the dialogue in pairs.
- Give the students a checklist to assess each other's spoken exchanges in a post office role play which they have recorded.

Extension activities

It is important that language skills and knowledge are recycled throughout a language program, and as students become confident with their performance, it is essential that they are extended. Extension can mean:
- introducing similar spoken interactions in different contexts
- increasing the complexity of the spoken interaction through:
  - increasing the length
  - increasing the number of interactants
  - introducing unpredictable or problematic elements into the discourse

– increasing the number of outcomes which have to be achieved through the discourse (eg having to post a number of different items going to different destinations)
- introducing a mixture of interactions (eg a service encounter with a phase of casual conversation)
- asking the students to perform outside the classroom
- transferring skills to other related texts or contexts.

Examples from a service encounter

Extension activities for a post office service encounter could include the following:

- Play tapes of problematic service encounters (eg when the customer has not heard the price or has not understood the options offered). Ask students to note how the customer asks for repetition or clarification.
- Ask students to role play a post office service encounter and introduce problematic elements such as a misunderstanding about destination etc.
- Organise for the students to write letters to people overseas or interstate and arrange for small groups to go to the post-office to mail them. Give the students a checklist to assess their own spoken exchanges at the post office.
- Ask students to role play a service encounter where they have to send a number of items all going to different overseas and interstate destinations.
- Ask students to compare a service encounter at the post-office with one at a fast food chain.
- Ask students to role play a service encounter in another context (eg hardware shop).

REVIEW

In this chapter we have looked at three different types of spoken texts which can be used in the classroom – scripted, semi-scripted and authentic. The characteristics of scripted texts and authentic discourse were contrasted and the necessity of introducing students to authentic texts was discussed.

We also presented a methodological framework which provides a way of systematising methodological decisions and emphasises the need for shifting responsibility in the classroom between teachers and students.

Finally, five categories of activities were presented with sample activities for developing speaking skills for a post office service encounter.

References

Brumfit, C. J. 1984. Cambridge: Cambridge University Press.
Burns, A. H. Joyce and S. Gollin. 1996. *I see what you mean. Using spoken discourse in the classroom: A handbook for teachers.* Sydney: NCELTR.
McCarthy, M. 1991. *Discourse analysis for language teachers.* Cambridge: Cambridge University Press.

Pearson D.P. and M.C. Gallagher 1983. The instruction of reading comprehension. *Contemporary Educational Psychology*, 8: 317–344.

Further reading

Beaverson, A. and C. Cartensen. 1983. *Starters dialogues*. Sydney: NCELTR.

Bygate, M. 1988. *Speaking*. Oxford: Oxford University Press.

Comfort, J, P. Rogerson, T. Stott and D Utley. 1994. *Speaking effectively: Developing skills for business English*. Cambridge: Cambridge University Press.

Cornish, S. 1992. *Community access : Curriculum guidelines*. Sydney: NSW AMES.

Cornish, S. and K. Brown, 1996. *Beach Street*. Sydney: NSW AMES.

Folse, K.S. 1996. *Discussion starters. Speaking fluency activities for advanced ESL/EFL students*. Ann Arbor: The University of Michigan Press.

Hello Australia. 1989. Sydney: NCELTR.

Joyce, H. 1992. *Workplace texts*. Sydney: NSW AMES.

Slade, D and L. Norris. 1986. *Teaching casual conversation*. Adelaide: National Curriculum Resource Centre.

CHAPTER

SEVEN

ASSESSING SPEAKING

PREREADING QUESTIONS

- How do you place students into classes within your teaching context?
- How do you go about assessing your students' speaking skills?
- What aspects of speaking do you assess?

Assessment is an integral aspect of the teaching-learning process and happens every day in the classroom as teachers continually make judgements about the performance of their students. Teachers use this information day to day to inform students about their progress as well as to evaluate the effectiveness of teaching materials and activities. However, information about student performance and progress is not confined to the immediate needs of the classroom. It is often used for purposes such as (Brindley 1989):

- accountability to funding providers
- passing on information about student achievement to other teachers
- providing articulated pathways of language development for students
- informing students about their progress through an overall language curriculum.

When we assess spoken language, we are interested either in how our students are likely to use language in social situations or in how well they have learnt what we have taught them. In most assessment situations we ask students to participate in an interview or an activity which will enable them to produce spoken language for us to assess. However, while a student is producing the spoken language it is difficult to focus on the range of features which go towards making a spoken interaction successful and so it is necessary to record student performances in order to assess them.

Assessing speaking skills is not a simple matter and spoken language assessment is a continuing focus for research and many books are written each year on assessment in language teaching.

Think about a particular student in your class.

1   What judgements did you make about this student's spoken language during the last lesson?
2   Who wants information about this student's performance beyond the classroom?

Spoken language assessment can be divided into two broad categories (Shohamy 1985), according to their purpose:

- assessment which predicts how a student will perform in a particular context
- assessment which relates to student performance in relation to a broad curriculum or a specific course.

The purpose for assessing a student's spoken language will influence the choice of assessment tools and the timing of the assessment. At the commencement of a course students are generally assessed to place them in an appropriate class or level, and at the end of a course students are generally assessed in terms of their achievement. However, students are also assessed throughout the teaching program with teachers assessing the performance of their students in every lesson. Both teachers and students, should see assessment as an integral part of the teaching-learning process.

In this Chapter we will examine the different types of spoken language assessment that occur at different points throughout a course. The main assessment types discussed are:

- proficiency assessment
- placement assessment
- diagnostic assessment
- formative assessment
- achievement assessment
- summative assessment.

These types of assessment often overlap; for example summative assessment, which occurs at the end of a course of study, may be a simple matter of undertaking an achievement assessment or it may involve collating all the formative assessments that have taken place through the course. This may be the case particularly where no formal achievement assessment is required. It is also possible that a thorough diagnostic assessment will be undertaken, if the time is available, as part of the placement assessment process.

Predicting future performance

In many contexts people want to have some idea of how second language learners will perform in particular educational or work situations.

Proficiency assessment

The aim of a proficiency assessment is to assess a person's level of language in relation to a specific future use. For example, tests have been developed to assess spoken language in relation to specific occupations such as taxi driving and teaching; or to specific education courses, for instance at a university.

Placement assessment

The aim of a placement assessment is to place students into an appropriate level within an institution or an overall course of study. Placement assessment is concerned with the student's present standing, and so relates to general ability rather than specific points of learning (Harrison 1983).

Some students may be placed in a particular class because they have achieved the requirements of a previous course – in this case placement is determined simply by stages of progression. However, if a student is entering an overall curriculum for the first time, it may be necessary to assess students for placement by referring to general descriptions such as beginner, post beginner, low intermediate, intermediate, upper intermediate, advanced. Some curricula may use the same categories but use different terminology such as level or stage. If students are placed on the basis of spoken language then each stage will be aligned to a spoken language level.

1 How are students placed into classes within your teaching institution?
2 What descriptions are used for the different levels?

Proficiency rating scales

Proficiency rating scales provide a general description of the learner and so can be used to place that person into a suitable level within an institution.

The Australian Second Language Proficiency Rating (ASLPR) scale is a nine-point proficiency rating scale in which 0 indicates no language proficiency and 5 is equivalent to a native speaker of English. In relation to various speaking, each of the nine points (0, 0+, 1-, 1, 1+, 2, 3, 4, 5) are described in terms of:

- extent of vocabulary
- grammar
- comprehensibility
- intonation and stress
- topics
- complexity of utterances
- self correction strategies.

Various aspects are outlined at each level and a general profile of a speaker at that particular level is provided. Figure 7.1 shows the spoken language profile descriptions at Level 3 of the ASLPR. The ASLPR, like all proficiency scales, aims to measure general language proficiency which is (Ingram and Wylie 1984: 125) 'the ability of the learner to carry out tasks in certain every situations in which we, as human beings, ...are necessarily involved.'

The oral interview

The most common procedure for assessing spoken language proficiency, particularly when using a proficiency rating scale, is through the oral interview. There are certain problems associated with oral interviews for assessment purposes. As Manidis and Prescott (1994: 26) point out:

> The oral proficiency interview is designed to elicit language behaviour for assessment. However since it is the rater who is in control of the encounter, the learner can offer only that language which the

interviewer/rater seeks. The rater has a clear responsibility to give the learner the opportunity to reach his or her linguistic ceiling and therefore must do as much as possible to elicit language.

There has been much research into the interview for assessment purposes. Suggestions about how the interviewer can elicit adequate language from the student have been made in relation to the staging of the interview and the types of procedures within the interview. Table 7.1 outlines the stage of the oral assessment interview and the role of the interviewer/assessor.

In order to make a more accurate assessment interviewers need to elicit adequate language by engaging students in conversation and asking open-ended questions. They can also use visual stimuli to prompt language interaction.

General Description	Examples of specific tasks (ESL)	Comment
S:2 Minimum social proficiency *Able to satisfy routine social demands and limited work requirements.* Can handle with confidence but not facility most social situations including introductions and casual conversations about current events, as well as work, family and autobiographical information. Has restricted register flexibility though, where a specialist register has been experienced, will have acquired some features of it. Has limited ability to vary the 'tone' of utterances. Can handle limited work requirements but will need help in handling any complications or difficulties. Hesitations are still frequent as the learner searches for vocabulary or grammar, but has a speaking vocabulary sufficient to express himself simply with circumlocutions on most topics pertinent to his everyday life; can usually handle elementary constructions quite accurately but does not have thorough or confident control of the grammar especially in longer constructions. Accent, though often quite faulty, is intelligible; undue exertion on the part of a native-speaking listener is not often necessary though some repetition in order to be understood may occur. Overall rate of utterance remains less than the native speaker's as a result of hesitations. Cohesion and discourse in short utterances or texts are secure but inconsistencies occur in longer ones.	Can give detailed information about own family, living conditions, educational background; can describe and converse on everyday things in his environment (e.g. his suburb, the weather); can describe present or most recent job or activity; can communicate on the spot with fellow workers or immediate superior (e.g. ask questions about job, make complaints about work conditions, time off etc.); can give simple messages over the telephone; can give directions and instructions for simple tasks in his everyday life (e.g. to tradesmen). Has tentative use of polite request forms, e.g. involving *could, would*. May sometimes offend by unintended blandness or aggressiveness, or irritate by over-deference where native speakers expect informality.	At this level, the learner's ability is sufficient to enable him to establish normal social relationships with native speakers.

Figure 7.1: Spoken language profile for ASPLR level 3 learner (Ingram and Wylie 1984: 50)

Stages	Procedure	Assessment
Exploratory	Welcome learner and introduce self. Explain purpose of interview. Initiate conversation.	Make an intuitive assessment
Analytical probing and extending	Elicit language samples by directing questions that allow the learner to display features of language behaviour described in the level you have selected.	Check level
	Extend depth of questions, use visual stimuli and change topics to seek extension of the language behaviour.	Adjust level (if necessary), check level
	Take learner to the point at which he/she can no longer function comfortably. Compare with previous level of interaction for conformation of level.	Confirm level
Concluding, winding down	Return to comfortable level of interaction for learner. Return to general conversation and proceed with remainder of assessment (e.g. reading and written language).	Record assessment

Figure 7.2: Stages and procedures of an oral assessment interview (Manidis and Prescott 1994: 27)

Assessing students' ongoing performance

Teachers are concerned with assessing student performance at various stages of a language program They are constantly assessing student performance in an informal way as lessons proceed, but in some language programs performance assessment may also be a formalised process leading to the award of a credential at the end of the course of study. In this section some of the assessment types generally used for assessing performance during a course are outlined.

Diagnostic assessment

Diagnostic assessment is used to identify a student's strengths and weaknesses or to diagnose specific learning difficulties which a student may have. The aim of diagnostic assessment is to gather information to allow for intervention in the learning process through the development of a program which is appropriate to the needs of students. Diagnostic assessment of a student's spoken language performance should be motivated by theoretical understandings of how spoken language is constructed. For example, knowledge of the genres that can occur within spoken language will enable the teacher to make clear statements about the student's ability to construct overall discourse. Knowledge of turn taking conventions will enable the teacher to make a clear assessment of the student's ability to control turn taking within a conversation.

Read Text 1, the transcript of a student's spoken language performance (taken from research data collected by NSW AMES). The student was asked to role play a telephone enquiry about joining the local library. What does the transcript reveal about the students' needs in relation to speaking?

Text 1
Transcript of roleplay enquiry to library
S = student L = librarian

S: Hello?

L: Good morning Bentwood Library.

S: Ah this is ah this is Luka speaking and ah I just moving ah from ah ah moving to this suburb and I … I want to know about ah library.

L: Yes?

S: How can I join … ah … to be a member?

L: Ah ha okay well you will need to come to the library itself and fill in a form.

S: Yeah um what do you need to join you?

L: Well ah if you bring um some form of ID um there's no fee at all, all we need is a proof of identity and ah the form and ah that's it.

S: Ah right it it needs no deposit or no no fee?

L: No no just ah we don't charge here.

S: All right and ah uh how many numbers of books as can I get at once?

L: All right yes you can borrow two books or cassettes at any one time.

S: Ah mean two books and two cassettes?

L: Well it could be one book and one cassette [or

S: [All right

L: A maximum of um of ah two books or cassettes.

S: Oh okay do you have any um magazines?

L: Yes but they're unfortunately we we ah we can't um make those available for borrowing but you can ah ah browse through them in the library itself.

S: Okay and ah if I if I late to return the books ah do you have any punishment or

L: Punishment? Well I wouldn't call it that but we do have penalties yes fifty a cents a day but we won't hit you or anything like that.

S: (laughing) Okay um and ah do you have any other other things for example video or CD or some.

L: Ah yes we have an extensive cassette collection, audio cassette collection and um not as many videos um and various other facilities for the public like a photo copier, a couple of computers um we're reasonably well resourced over here

S: Ah so I can use anytime ah.

L: Well during the opening hours obviously yes.

S: Oh so and ah ah um its your ah your can I can tell can you tell me the opening hours?

L: Opening time?

S: Yes

L: Yes we're open Mondays to Fridays from nine o'clock until ah six o'clock

S: To six o'clock. Okay.

L: And on weekends if you're interested as well.

S: Okay.

L: Are you?

S: Then thank you very much.

The transcript in Text 1 can be used for diagnostic analysis of the student's spoken language needs and for making decisions about follow-up activities, as demonstrated in Table 7.1.

Formative assessment

Formative assessment occurs throughout a course and is an integral part of teaching and learning in good teaching programs. It informs teachers about student progress and whether there is a need to revise and modify the course in any way. It is essentially undertaken to monitor student learning and how they are managing particular tasks in the classroom. It also informs students about their progress and what they should be doing to improve their language. Within the classroom, diagnostic and formative assessment are generally closely aligned.

Think about your current course or one you have taught previously.

1 What formative assessments did you undertake?
2 What decisions did you make about the direction of your course as a result of these assessments?

Table 7.1: Diagnostic analysis of Text 1

Diagnostic assessment	Teaching implications
overall failure to develop discourse in conjunction with the other interactant – student discourse reveals she has asked a number of rehearsed questions	Model native speaker text and indicate stages of discourse which are developed by response to cues from other interactants
past perfect tense *I just moving into* > I've just moved into	Provide input and guided practice on alternative tense forms of verbs
use of articles *I want to know about library* > I want to know about the library	Provide practice on use of definite articles – drill and guided practice
vocabulary problems *deposit* > fee *punishment* > penalty clarification strategy – question *Ah mean two books and two cassettes* > Do you mean two books and two cassettes?	Design vocabulary building exercises on bureaucratic terms (eg fees etc) Provide input and practice in clarification strategies
conditional *If I late to return the books* > If I return books late	Provide input and practice on conditional structures and relevant verb forms
use of pronoun as reference *Ah so I I can use anytime* > Ah so I can use it anytime?	Provide guided practice on pronoun referencing
failure to pick up on discourse cue twice L: *And on weekends if you're interested as well* S: *Okay* L: *Are you?* S: *Then thank you very much*	Use transcript to indicate failure to pick up on cues Discuss the tenor implications of ignoring the librarian's cue and how she might interpret this Provide listening activities on discourse strategies

Achievement and summative assessment

Achievement assessment is concerned with what a student has learnt in a language course. With increased accountability beyond the classroom, achievement assessment has become formalised in many teaching contexts and often leads to the awarding of credentials. Achievement assessment is also used to give students some idea of their overall progress and to decide on where they should go next. It can be an ongoing procedure throughout a course and at the end can form the basis of

summative assessment, which is essentially concerned with how well students performed in relation to the aims and objectives of the course.

Criterion referenced and norm referenced assessment

Traditional approaches to assessment have been based on norm referenced assessment where student performances are graded in relation to one another along a scale. This is often the case in formal language examinations.

In all sectors of education, over recent years, there has been a move towards criterion-referenced assessment. Criterion-referenced assessment (CRA) is based on specific assessment criteria that have been outlined for the performance of a specific task. The teacher assesses each individual student performance against these criteria. CRA is not concerned with rating one student performance against another.

Figure 7.3 is an example of criterion-referenced assessment. It is a description of a competency outlined in the NSW AMES Certificate in Spoken and Written English II. In the second column there are a number of performance criteria which the teacher uses to assess each student's performance.

Competency 5 Can give spoken instructions

Elements	Performance Criteria	Range Statements	Evidence Guide **Sample Tasks**
i. can give spoken instructions in correct sequence ii. can respond to requests for repetition or clarification as required iii. can use appropriate vocabulary iv. can structure imperative clauses	• gives spoken instructions in correct sequence • responds to requests for repetition or clarification as requred • uses appropriate vocabulary • structures imperative clauses	• familiar field • approximately 5 instructions • face-to-face • telephone for Distance Learning students • sympathetic interlocutor	• Learner gives instructions on how to use a machine eg. photocopier, vending machine • Learner gives known destinations.

Phonology

Specific performance criteria related to phonology have not been included. However it is assumed that:
• articulation of some phonemes and clusters as well as intonation, stress and rhythm in longer phrases and clauses may often be innaccurate or unconventional
• teaching programs will pay attention to:
   – phonological features of longer utterances
   – developing learner self-monitoring and repair/correction strategies

---

Figure 7.3: Example of a criterion-referenced assessment (Certificate in Spoken and Written English II 1995)

You are teaching a course in a workplace which aims to improve student telephone skills at work. You have been teaching the students how to leave messages when they call other departments within the workplace.

What criteria would you outline to assess a roleplay where the students have to phone another department and leave a message for someone who is not available.

One advantage of criterion-referenced assessment is that the performance criteria can be shared with the learners throughout the teaching process. In this way the goal for language performance can be made clear and the students do not have to second guess how the teacher will be assessing them. They can also use the criteria to monitor their own performance as well as that of their peers.

Case study: Criterion-referenced assessment

A teacher was delivering a course for engineers whose first language was not English. The engineers were reporting difficulties in dealing with various situations in the English speaking workplace. They were particularly concerned with difficulties they were experiencing over the telephone. The teacher developed a number of units centred around using the telephone which included:

- Leaving messages
- Taking messages
- Placing an order with an external organisation
- Phoning in from the field to explain procedures and problems
- Checking specifications with personnel in other departments.

The teacher was concerned that the engineers should transfer the spoken language skills they practised in the classroom to their work contexts so she organised for various workplace personnel to cooperate in roleplays with the students. In one instance she organised for a student to telephone a supervisor and leave a message for someone who was not available. The telephone conversation was recorded. She gave the student and the supervisor the following set of criteria for making judgements about the student's performance:

- opens conversation appropriately
- requests to speak to the required person
- asks when person will be back
- requests to leave a message
- identifies self
- orders information in logical sequence
- spells own name clearly
- leaves telephone number clearly
- checks information is understood
- closes conversation appropriately.

111

Table 7.2: Assessment principles relevant to assessment of spoken discourse

Criteria	Comments
Assessment criteria must be made explicit to the students	Criteria should be explained to students in language adapted to their level.
Students must be informed that they are being assessed	This is ideal, but it does affect student performance if they know a specific task is to be assessed. A compromise position is to inform students that assessments will take place regularly throughout a course, without notifying them of specific tasks.
The method of assessment must be explained to the students in language adapted to their level	This should be discussed at the beginning of a course as part of overall orientation The method of assessment should be discussed in terms of the educational context of the institution (eg if the institution adopts competency-based assessment then this should be explained.
Assessment must relate back to the aims and objectives of the program	Assessment will be facilitated if objectives are couched in terms of what students should be able to do at the end of the course or teaching sequence.
Assessment must be reliable	Assessment should be consistent in two ways: • the same assessor should rate several task performances at the same standard (intra-rater reliability) • several assessors should reach agreement about the same task performance (inter-rater reliability).
Assessment must be valid	To be valid an assessment task must: • assess what it claims to assess (eg assessing skills in spoken discourse should not depend on a student's ability to write) • assess what has been taught (content validity).
Assessment must be reported in terms of a common language about achievement comparable across the organisation	If other teachers, curriculum writers and program managers are to understand statements about achievement, they must use common and shared descriptions.

Assessment principles

The focus on assessment in recent years has led to a consideration of assessment principles. These principles, as they apply to the assessment of spoken discourse, are outlined in Table 7.2 (from Burns, Joyce and Gollin 1996: 91–2).

REVIEW

In this chapter we have examined the different purposes for assessing spoken language and outlined the following types of assessment which can occur throughout a language program:
• proficiency assessment
• placement assessment
• diagnostic assessment
• formative assessment
• achievement assessment
• summative assessment.

The chapter also examined proficiency ratings scales, the oral language assessment interview and criterion referenced assessment.

References

Brindley, G. 1989. *Assessing achievement in the learner-centred curriculum. Sydney*. NCELTR, Macquarie University.
Certificates I, II, III and IV. 1995. Sydney: NSW AMES.
Burns, A., H. Joyce and S. Gollin. 1996. *I see what you mean. Using spoken discourse in the classroom: A handbook for teachers*. Sydney: NCELTR.
Harrison, J. 1983. *A language testing handbook*. London: Macmillan.
Ingram, D. and E. Wylie. 1984. Australian Second Language *Proficiency Ratings*. Canberra: AGPS.
Manidis, M. and P Prescott. 1994. *Assessing oral language proficiency: A handbook for teachers in the Adult Migrant English Program*. Sydney: NCELTR.
Shohamy, E, 1985 *A practical handbook in language testing for the second language teacher*. Israel: Tel Aviv University.

Further reading

Brindley, G. 1985. *The assessment of second language proficiency: Issues and approaches*. Adelaide: National Curriculum Resource Centre.
Brindley, G. 1995. *Language assessment in action*. Sydney: NCELTR.
Christie, J. and S. Delaruelle. (forthcoming). *Assessment and moderation*. Sydney: NSW AMES and NCELTR.
Derewianka, B. 1992. *Language assessment in primary classrooms*. Sydney: Harcourt Brace Jovanivich.
Genessee, F. and J. A. Upshur. 1996. *Classroom-based evaluation in second language education*. Cambridge: Cambridge University Press.
Weir, C. 1993. *Understanding and developing language tests*. Hemel Hempstead: Prentice Hall.

EIGHT

COMMON QUESTIONS ABOUT SPEAKING

The questions in this chapter have been gathered from those with whom we have worked in preservice and inservice courses where teaching speaking in communicative language classrooms has been a major topic. They represent issues which have emerged for these teachers as they have planned lessons for teaching speaking to learners at various levels of ability. The questions are not sequenced in any particular order and are presented for readers who may have asked themselves similar questions.

The questions also extend or summarise some of the main ideas about teaching speaking which have been discussed in this book and raise other issues which readers may wish to reflect on further. Suggestions for further reading are provided for those wishing to explore these topics in more detail.

Before you begin reading, you may wish to reflect on your own responses to the ten questions we consider in this chapter:

1　How do I teach beginners?
2　How much English should the teacher use in the EFL classroom?
3　Should I teach speaking, listening, reading and writing separately?
4　How do I teach the language features of spoken texts?
5　How should I teach pronunciation?
6　How do I teach students in mixed-level groups?
7　Should I focus on developing fluency or accuracy?
8　How can I encourage students to practise speaking outside the classroom?
9　What should I do when students are reluctant to speak in class?
10　How do I integrate speaking and listening?

1
How do I teach beginners?

Our initial response to this question is to ask another question: What do we mean by a beginner? Some writers would claim that there is no such thing as a real beginner as it is likely that most students will have had at least some minimal exposure to English.

A useful starting point is to consider the variations in language learning skills and resources that beginner learners will bring with them to the classroom. Students may:

- be complete beginners
- be *false* beginners; that is people who have had some limited experiences of learning English or who have picked up or taught themselves some English
- have had quite extensive experiences of learning English in the past but may have had no further need to use the language
- be highly educated and have learned English mainly through the medium of writing
- have had little or no formal education so will have few first language literacy skills to assist them with second language learning.

There are also other factors that may influence beginner learning that teachers need to take into account, such as:

- the institutional arrangements in which learning is taking place
- learners' access to English speakers for additional practice
- the learners' cultural attitudes towards the language and towards the target culture
- the relative similarities or differences between the learner's first language and English, including differences in script
- the learning strategies, anxiety and motivation of the learners.

It is very important that learners are given a great deal of contextual support in the initial stages of learning to speak (see Chapter 1 and 2). Their understanding of the new language will be greatly increased if classroom discussions and tasks involve the use of aids, such as pictures, photographs, videos, familiar objects or *realia*, gestures and concrete or hands-on demonstrations, which relate to the topic or text being taught. It is also important that students are made aware of the contexts in which the language being presented occurs. This awareness can be increased through shared activities such as:

- excursions
- practical tasks (eg following instructions for making things)
- visual representations (eg posters)
- team games.

Listening activities that are contextualised, and that draw on learner expectations and previous experiences, are particularly important and help to develop confidence at beginner stages of speaking. In order to develop their speaking skills students need to familiarise themselves with the sound, rhythm and intonation patterns of English (see Question 5) and to relate what they are hearing to concepts which are meaningful. Listening and speaking activities should be integrated (see Question 3), rather than taught as separate skills so that vocabulary and structures are recycled across different tasks and learners have an opportunity to consolidate their learning. Integration and recycling through a range of spoken and written tasks on the same topic are important so that learners are not overloaded with too many different language structures and texts to deal with at the same time (see Green 1992 for a model of an integrated unit of work for beginners).

One of the greatest challenges for beginner learners is to build a sufficient vocabulary so that they can begin to talk about a topic or to use language appropriately within a particular context. Activities which help them to build a vocabulary field are extremely valuable (see Chapter 3); however, it is important to remember that these vocabulary activities should be a means of working towards the use of more complete spoken texts. Learning individual vocabulary items is necessary but insufficient if learners are to transfer their speaking skills beyond the classroom.

As we pointed out in Chapter 2, native speakers often use formulaic expressions, or set *chunks* of language in familiar and routine situations. These expressions can be particularly helpful for beginners who can be encouraged to learn formulaic expressions which will be useful inside the classroom (eg *I don't understand; can you repeat that, please*) as well as outside (eg *Hello, how are you?; See you soon)*.

It is helpful to present beginner learners with simple, spoken interactions rather than more complex ones. For example, the stages of the service encounter genre can be provided in its reduced and predictable form, with more complex or unpredictable stages being introduced at a later stage as learners gain greater proficiency. In the early stages, semi-scripted texts are easier for learners to process than completely unscripted samples of native speaker interaction. Beginning with more teacher-controlled preparation exercises (see Chapter 6) can provide students with a model of a proficient speaker and allow them to rehearse language forms and functions. Again, as students become more confident and more proficient, more learner-centred extension activities such as roleplays, games and problem-solving tasks can be provided.

Learners can be introduced from the earliest stages to *learning to learn* strategies which will help to make their language learning more efficient and productive. This may mean introducing them to classroom study routines such as organising and categorising their materials or using a learner's dictionary, as well as raising their awareness of how to seek opportunities to practise their speaking skills outside the classroom.

Further reading

Ellis, G. and B. Sinclair. 1989. *Learning to learn English*. Cambridge: Cambridge University Press.

Grundy, P. 1994. *Beginners*. Oxford: Oxford University Press.

Green, J. 1992. *Making the links. Video and workbook*. Melbourne: AMES, Victoria.

Jackson, E. 1993. *Non-language outcomes in the language classroom: Curriculum guidelines*. Sydney. NCELTR and NSW AMES.

Jackson, E. 1994. *Non-language outcomes: Activities and resources*. Sydney: NCELTR and NSW AMES.

Nunan, D. and J. Burton (eds). 1989. *National Curriculum Project Framework: New arrivals: Initial elementary proficiency*. Sydney: NCELTR.

Ramm. J. *Learners with minimal formal education*. Melbourne: AMES, Victoria.

Willing, K. 1989. *Teaching how to learn: Learning strategies in ESL*. Sydney: NCELTR.

2

How much English should the teacher use in the EFL classroom?

English language classes are conducted in many different institutional settings and the extent to which students are able to hear and speak English outside the classroom will vary considerably. In Australia, language learners have many opportunities to practise their English outside the classroom and the majority of English teachers will conduct classes at all levels predominantly through the medium of English . Where teachers have bilingual skills, they may also use their knowledge of another language to assist their learners, although it is generally the case that both EFL and ESL classes in Australia are made up of students from many different language backgrounds.

When English is taught in a country where it is not the main language, the situation for teachers is very different. The students and the teacher are likely to share a common language other than English and the teacher will need to make decisions about the amount of English to be used. To some extent these decisions will depend upon the kind of curriculum approach that is taken, the objectives of the program and the level of the students. However, it is generally agreed that the use of the target language itself, rather than teaching the second language through the medium of the first, is an important consideration in student progress.

The type of activities that are presented to facilitate speaking are a further factor. If tasks for speaking depend mainly on learning vocabulary, drilling language patterns and reading simple dialogues, it is unlikely that learners will acquire a broad range of communicative skills that will enable them to operate effectively in more complex language situations. It is important, therefore that teachers draw on a wide variety of tasks and materials. These may include more formal language learning tasks and materials, such as course books and audio tapes prepared specifically for language learning, as well as authentic resources from the context in which the language is being taught. In this way learners will be exposed to a mixture of tasks and materials and will be able to move from structured language production to more communicative language use.

Possible strategies for increasing the use of the target language include:
- using the target language as often as possible in order to provide realistic models for students
- drawing on other English speaking colleagues or native speakers where feasible to provide models of spoken interactions
- developing a flexible approach based on careful considerations of where, when and why to choose the target language rather than the first language and vice versa

- using the target language whenever possible for classroom instructions and interaction, especially as this provides a highly contextualised use of language
- monitoring situations where explanations in the target language become too complex for learners and using the first language to provide more comprehensible explanations
- designing communicative tasks which follow on from structured presentation and practice.

Further reading

O'Grady, C. 1989. *A bilingual approach to teaching English to adult migrants: A handbook for teachers*. Sydney. NSW AMES.

Willis, J. 1981. *Teaching English through English*. London: Longman.

3

Should I teach speaking, listening, reading and writing separately?

In the more traditional approaches to language teaching which were described in Chapter 3, the macroskills of speaking, listening, reading and writing were frequently taught separately. It was also sometimes considered beneficial to introduce them in a relatively fixed order. This separation of skills is reflected in some timetables for language teaching programs. However, if we reflect on the way we use language in our daily lives, it is easy to see that language skills are not used in isolation. They operate together in different contexts to fulfil different social purposes (see Chapter 1). If we agree with the argument that the role of the language classroom is to equip students with language skills which they can use in and beyond the classroom context, then we will need to give them tasks which help them to understand how different language skills are related.

When planning for an integrated approach, it is useful to consider how events may take place and relate to each other in daily situations (see Chapter 5). This approach can involve a quite limited integration of skills or it can introduce much longer sequences of events. The choice will depend on the focus of the program and the learners.

An example of a more limited situation is one in which students are asked to obtain some information over the telephone about the opening times of a library. This would involve:

• looking up the telephone number in the directory
• writing down the number on a notepad
• dialling the number
• initiating the call and requesting the information
• listening to the information
• writing down the opening times on a notepad
• reading the times at a later time when needed.

A more protracted language event would include a complex sequence of skills; for example, still using the topic of libraries, it might involve:

• finding the opening times of the library
• going to the library to enquire about joining
• reading information about membership and filling in a membership application
• returning the application to the library
• enquiring about the availability of certain books
• selecting and borrowing books
• reading the borrowed books
• returning the books to the library
• discussing the books with friends.

These natural sequences of tasks can provide a framework for program planning which integrates different language skills in a similar way to the way they are integrated outside the classroom. This allows us to analyse which skills will need to be emphasised at each point and how the language used in the development of one skill may be recycled and practised again for another skill. It also allows us to identify where we may need to focus on developing spoken language forms and functions rather than written language forms and functions. This approach can help learners to discuss and understand how different language skills interact and also how they are used appropriately and effectively in a particular context.

It is possible to introduce more unpredictable elements of situations gradually as students become more competent. In the first library sequence outlined above, the caller may be told to hold on, be placed in a queue or be given the information by a recorded message. In the second library sequence, the borrower may be told that the books are not available, that they are on a restricted loan or that there is an overdue fine which must be paid.

Some learners will need to develop particular language skills, and the focus of the program may be designed to emphasise those skills. It is still useful, however, to monitor how the spoken and written tasks can be integrated; for example although a conversation class may be conducted to develop greater fluency for students who have well developed second language literacy skills it might still involve the use of written texts and materials. In a literacy class tasks need to extend and reinforce skills in a way that relates logically to language use outside the classroom, including the use of spoken language.

Further reading

Bell, J. 1990. *Integrated skills: Upper intermediate*. Oxford: Heinemann.
Burns, A., H. Joyce and S. Gollin. 1996. *'I see what you mean' Teaching spoken discourse in the classroom: A handbook for teachers*. Sydney: NCELTR.
Byrne, D. 1981. Integrating skills. In K. Johnson and K. Morrow (eds). *Communication in the classroom*. London: Longman.
Joyce, H. 1992. *Workplace texts*. Sydney: NSW AMES.
Hood, S., N. Solomon and A. Burns. 1996. *Focus on reading*. Sydney: NCELTR.
McDonough, J. and C. Shaw. 1993. *Materials and methods in ELT*. Oxford: Blackwell.

4

How do I teach the language features of spoken texts?

In Chapter 1 we looked at some of the differences between spoken and written language. We suggested that it is important for students to have an understanding of the typical grammatical features of spoken texts and for these to be discussed and taught explicitly. The point of teaching spoken language, particularly through the introduction of authentic dialogues, is to enable students to interact with speakers of English in different social situations.

Depending on the level of the students and the nature of the interaction, you will probably decide to focus on different features of spoken texts as with most students it will not be possible to deal with all aspects of an interaction in the same lesson. It is useful, therefore, to reintroduce dialogues and focus on different aspects in subsequent lessons. If students are made familiar with some of the general features of spoken discourse, they will be able to compare different interactions.

In Chapters 1 and 2 we highlighted some of the typical features of spoken discourse that can be discussed with students, including:
- discourse structure
- openings and closings
- turn taking, turn giving, turn allocating and turn keeping
- asking and answering questions
- making statements and offers
- topic shifts.

There are a number of teaching strategies that can be utilised when focusing on the language features of spoken texts including:
- contextualising language features by teaching them in relation to the spoken texts in your program
- analysing the texts with the whole class and focusing explicitly on the grammatical features
- constructing spoken texts jointly with the whole class or with groups of students and focusing on grammar as part of text production
- developing grammatical exercises which assist students to practise the grammatical features they need to produce effective texts
- reworking written texts into spoken texts and vice versa which will focus student attention on how grammar changes in this process.

A further issue to consider in teaching the language features of spoken texts is *appropriacy*; that is, knowing how to use spoken language relevantly and effectively in a given situation. This knowledge involves an understanding of appropriate *register*. Although this term is familiar to language teachers it has generally been interpreted as referring to either informal or formal language. However, analysis which has been developed through systemic functional linguistics (see Chapter 3) provides a more extensive view of register and how it relates to social contexts. Put simply, register is the variety of language which is used in a particular social situation. It results from three variables within any situation which constrain the language choices speakers and writers make in the construction of texts (Halliday 1985):

Field: is concerned with what is going on in the context and what people are talking about. It is the topic of conversation.

Tenor: is concerned with who is taking part in the conversation and their social relationship.

Mode: is concerned with what part language is playing in the context and what the interactants are expecting language to do.

It is valuable to give students insights into how these three variables work together in language use and how they determine the language we select in a social situation as it provides them with a framework for listening and producing spoken discourse.

Further reading

Burns, A., H. Joyce and S. Gollin. 1996. *I see what you mean. Using spoken discourse in the classroom: A handbook for teachers.* Sydney: NCELTR.

Butt, D., R Fahey, S. Spinks and C. Yallop. 1995. *Using functional grammar: An explorer's guide.* Sydney: NCELTR.

Eggins, S. 1994. *An introduction to systemic functional linguistics.* London: Pinter.

Halliday, M.A.K. 1985. *An introduction to functional grammar.* London: Edward Arnold.

Hammond, J., A. Burns, H. Joyce, D. Brosnan and L. Gerot. 1992. *English for social purposes.* Sydney: NCELTR.

5
How should I teach pronunciation?

Pronunciation is, without doubt, an integral feature of learning to speak a language, and important pronunciation features such as stress, rhythm and intonation contribute significantly to the development of meaning. While those learning a second language at an early age are at an advantage when attempting to develop more native-like pronunciation, older language learners usually experience difficultly in adapting their pronunciation to the sound patterns of a new language. If a student has good grammar, but poor pronunciation, conversations with native speakers are likely to be very limited. It is important to remember, however, that in language learning the main aim is to enable learners to achieve intelligibility rather than native-like pronunciation.

The amount of time spent on pronunciation will depend on the degree of mastery of the sound system your learners display. As far as possible, it is preferable to integrate pronunciation work with the range of speaking tasks your learners will undertake. This means providing activities for particular aspects of pronunciation as a component of the spoken interactions and contexts you are teaching and not as isolated and separate exercises in themselves.

It is important for learners, especially at beginning levels, to be given assistance in mastering the sounds of the new language and to have time in class to focus on pronunciation. Word stress (the pattern of stressed syllables in words) and intonation (the rising and falling levels of pitch used across utterances) are particularly important for beginners as they contribute significantly to meaning and play a very important role in how we listen to one another. Intonation should be included in the teaching of speaking at all levels. Lower level learners need to have practice in listening to native speaker intonation and more advanced learners need to tune in to the subtleties of meaning which are carried by intonation.

During classroom activities, it is important for learners to know when the teacher is switching from a focus on pronunciation to a focus on meaning. Focusing on pronunciation does not necessarily imply simultaneously focusing on meaning, and it can often be disconcerting for students, especially those at lower levels, to move from one focus to the other without prior warning. We can make these differences in emphasis easier for learners to understand if we differentiate clearly and explicitly between different segments of our teaching. They will then be aware of when we want them to concentrate on accuracy of pronunciation and when we are concerned with fluency of discourse.

The following strategies can be used to integrate pronunciation into lessons:

- identify sounds which may be new or different for some learners and help them to practise these where necessary
- raise learner awareness of key aspects of English pronunciation such as word and sentence stress, rhythm and intonation which may not be present in their own languages
- provide listening activities, related to the context or topic you are teaching, that involve native speaker interactions in order to provide models for pronunciation
- use transcripts of native speaker interactions to develop activities which focus on key aspects of pronunciation
- integrate pronunciation work with particular aspects of speaking you are introducing to your learners (eg vocabulary building, practising formulaic expressions, asking for clarification)
- provide additional practice or, if possible, referral to special pronunciation classes, tutor support or individual learning centres for learners whose pronunciation is seriously impeding their intelligibility
- encourage learners to monitor their own pronunciation by listening to native speech outside the classroom and to raise their own pronunciation issues for classroom discussion.

Further reading

Dalton, C. and B. Seidlhofer. 1994. *Pronunciation*. Oxford: Oxford University Press.

Kenworthy, J. 1987. *Teaching English pronunciation*. London: Longman.

Leroy, C. 1995. *Pronunciation. Resource Books for Language Teachers*. Oxford: Oxford University Press.

Morley, J. (ed.). 1987. *Current perspectives on pronunciation: Practices anchored in theory*. Washington, D.C.: TESOL.

Zawadski, H. 1992. *In tempo*. Sydney: NCELTR.

Yallop, C. 1995. *English phonology*. Sydney: NCELTR.

6
How do I teach students in mixed-level groups?

Many teachers find themselves teaching classes where students have a very wide range of different characteristics and language learning needs. Even in homogeneous classes where students may have been placed according to common criteria, different learning styles and attitudes towards learning will often mean that learners progress at different rates. Learner differences in mixed level groups may include:

- variations in spoken proficiency levels
- gaps between spoken and written language skills
- a variety of language and cultural backgrounds
- a wide range of previous educational experiences
- different levels of formal and informal exposure to English
- variations in access to English outside the classroom.

When faced with such differences, teachers may feel that their students have been placed in a situation which is not conducive to the most effective language learning. However, some recent Australian research (Burns and Hood 1997) has indicated that students view mixed-level groups very positively. They generally feel that they have greater scope to draw on the range of skills and learning strategies presented within the group. They also value positive group dynamics and their roles and relationships within the classroom community. Spoken interactions within disparate groups may also be more genuinely communicative as learners draw on individual resources to negotiate meaning with each other.

Some teachers have reported that teaching mixed-level groups has the advantage of making them more aware of their students' individual differences. This leads to a deeper analysis of the specific strengths and weaknesses of each student which can then be used as the basis for classroom planning and for making clearer decisions about learner groupings for different kinds of tasks. It also raises awareness of the importance of discussing individual learning strategies with students and of encouraging them to take some responsibility for learning.

However, while it is valuable to be aware of individual learning differences and needs, it is usually impractical for language teachers to develop individual lesson plans for each student. Nor is it necessary to divide the class into fixed proficiency groupings which remain constant throughout the course and which involve the teacher in developing totally different programs. The strategies listed below provide a starting point for assisting a mixed-level group with spoken language development:

- depending on the purpose of the task, group or pair students according to different criteria (eg first language, gender, proficiency level, self-selection) to support and assist each other

- draw on more advanced students to discuss with the whole class comparisons between first language and English in terms of discourse structure and strategies, grammatical features and pronunciation
- use role play to model spoken interactions for all learners and to provide the basis for introducing unpredictable stages in interaction for more advanced learners
- build up shared classroom language and provide classroom explanations which model how tasks are to be carried out
- organise shared learning experiences such as excursions, practical classroom activities, social events or visitors which enable all learners to participate and provide a basis for extension tasks for more advanced learners
- use common sets of materials (eg audio tapes, videos and scripted and unscripted dialogues) to develop tasks at different levels
- involve the whole class in discussions about situations for using English outside the classroom and encourage them to share their strategies
- provide opportunities, where possible, for learners to access self-paced activities, either through individual learning centres or individual learning contracts.

Further reading

Burns, A. and S. Hood (eds). Forthcoming. *Teachers' Voices 2: Teaching disparate learner groups.* Sydney: NCELTR.

Dingle, N. (ed). 1994. *Teaching multi-focus language classes.* Brisbane: TAFE Queensland Language Services.

Hadfield, J. 1993. *Classroom dynamics.* Melbourne: Oxford University Press.

Prodromou, L. 1992. *Mixed ability classes.* London: Macmillan.

7
Should I focus on developing fluency or accuracy?

In the days when language teaching approaches were only concerned with grammatical and structural accuracy, the question of whether teachers should focus on fluency or accuracy was not an issue. The introduction of communicative language teaching approaches, however, has meant that students are encouraged to develop fluent communication skills as well as being introduced to correct grammatical forms (see Chapter 3). In a communicative model the concept of accuracy itself becomes broader, as it is no longer a matter of just using correct grammatical forms, but also depends on an understanding of appropriate responses in different social contexts.

Teachers will need to consider a number of issues when deciding whether to emphasise fluency or accuracy. In the first place the decision depends on the objectives of the program or lesson, and the purposes for which learners engage in the activities associated with that lesson. There will clearly be occasions where we want our students to understand and practise as correctly as possible new discourse patterns, language items or structures, such as when students are preparing for:

- tests or assessments
- non-classroom contexts, such as work or academic settings and situations, where they will be expected to produce more accurate language.

When we are introducing learners to a new context or topic, we may wish to focus on giving them the discourse patterns and grammatical structures which will enable them to speak in the new context or about the new topic. We may wish to teach them:

- new vocabulary items
- formulaic expressions associated with the text type (eg *I wonder if you could help me*)
- typical verb patterns related to the topic (eg action verbs related to the topic or verbs of thinking, having, feeling)
- expressions for time, frequency, place or location (eg *seven thirty at night, several times a month, behind the bank*)
- expressions for fulfilling particular language functions (eg giving or asking for advice)
- relevant discourse strategies (eg asking for clarification, asking for repetition).

Classroom tasks of this nature are sometimes referred to as *pre-communicative* (Littlewood 1981) or *skill-getting* tasks (Rivers and Temperley 1978). They can also be called *pedagogic* tasks as they are more concerned with providing input for the teaching-learning process, than with giving learners opportunities to rehearse language for out-of-class use. In these kinds of activities, learners should be encouraged to be as accurate as possible.

At other times, we will want students to concentrate on using the language they have learned without being inhibited by demands for accuracy. We may, for instance, want the learners to be able to practise their communicative skills in relation to contexts or topics. For example, we may want them to complete a role-play on the topic of public transport in which they have to ask for directions or to make a timetable enquiry successfully. We are also likely to emphasise fluency more than accuracy when asking students to complete an *opinion gap* task where they have to debate alternative solutions to a problem or a *jigsaw task* where they have to collaborate by providing different pieces of information to complete the activity.

These kinds of activities have been termed *communicative* (Littlewood 1981) or *skill-using* (Rivers and Temperley 1978) activities. They can also be thought of as more *authentic* tasks as they are most concerned with approximating or reproducing the kinds of out-of-class interactions that learners may find themselves in. In these circumstances, we will be aiming for fluency rather than accuracy so that learners can practise developing speaking skills which are transferable to social situations. At the same time, of course, the teacher will be aiming to monitor the learner success in speaking about these topics and will be making decisions about the vocabulary, structures or discourse strategies which may need to be retaught or reinforced through further classroom tasks.

It is probably most useful, as Brumfit (1984) suggests, to see accuracy and fluency as complementary rather than contrary and to make conscious decisions about when to use activities, such as drills or substitution exercises, which allow students to develop their skills in language *form* and when to use less teacher-controlled activities, such as role plays, where the objective will be to encourage *fluency* and *communication skills*.

Further reading

Brumfit, C. 1984. *Communicative methodology in language teaching*. Cambridge: Cambridge University Press.

Harmer, J. 1992. *The practice of English language teaching*. New edition. London: Longman.

Littlewood, W.T. 1981. *Communicative language teaching - An introduction*. Cambridge: Cambridge University Press.

Nunan, D. 1991. *Language teaching methodology*. Hemel Hempstead: Prentice Hall.

Rivers, W. and M. Temperley. 1978. *A practical guide to the teaching of English as a foreign or second language*. New York: Oxford University Press.

8

How can I encourage students to practise speaking outside the classroom?

The extent to which students are able to practise speaking outside the classroom will, of course, vary according to whether they are learning English in a country where it is spoken or learning it as a foreign language. However, even when students are learning in countries where English is not spoken, it is often possible for them to encounter English expressions on television, in newspapers and in other media. Native speakers can also be invited to the classroom to interact with the students and the teacher and this can provide models of native speaker interaction. In this way, students begin to get a sense of how English is used for communicative purposes.

In countries like Australia, where English is spoken, teachers sometimes comment that their students seem reluctant to practise their English outside the classroom. There may be any number of social and cultural factors which account for this situation and it is valuable for teachers to spend some time researching with their students where and why they need to speak English and the difficulties that may be encountered. Factors accounting for limited English practise outside the classroom may include:

- lack of contact with native speakers
- dependence on other family members who may undertake interactions in English on their behalf
- lack of confidence or motivation
- previous negative experiences in using English
- cultural factors based on religion, gender or age.

Investigating factors of this kind provides the teacher with a clearer picture of strategies which can be developed to facilitate use of English outside the classroom. Some of the following strategies may be useful:

- discuss with students the benefits of practising English outside the classroom as a way of developing their own learning strategies and of making progress in English
- help students to identify contexts where they need to interact with English speakers and practise the spoken language they need to use in these contexts
- ask students to keep a record over a short period of time of all the situations where they would have liked to speak English, and use this to provide structured tasks which relate to specific discourse features (eg greetings, taking turns etc)
- provide speaking tasks to be completed outside the classroom which are an extension of classwork (eg phoning the railway station to find the times of trains after practising this in a unit of work on transport)
- enlist the help of other teachers or sympathetic friends who can be called upon to help students practise non-classroom tasks (eg students could make a telephone call to another teacher)

- set aside times for students to report on their experiences with out-of-class tasks
- encourage students to practise genuine communicative tasks within the teaching centre (eg interacting with students from other language background during breaks or contacting the centre to indicate absence from class)
- use real situations experienced by students to develop a problem-solving approach and to discuss discourse strategies which could be used to communicate more effectively in similar contexts.

Further reading

Auerbach, E. and N. Wallerstein. 1986. *ESL for action. Problem posing at work*. Reading, Mass: Addison Wesley:

Kohn, J. Forthcoming. Using English outside the classroom. In A. Burns, and S. Hood. (eds).*Teachers' voices 2: Teaching disparate learners*. Sydney: NCELTR.

9

What should I do when students are reluctant to speak in class?

There are many reasons why students may be reluctant to participate in classroom tasks which involve speaking, and they may have more to do with the task of second language learning in general than with spoken language in particular.

Learners unwillingness to participate in spoken tasks may be due to cultural factors, for example:
- a belief that learning involves listening to the teacher and not actively speaking up in class
- a belief that language learning is based primarily on reading and writing from a text book and completing written exercises
- unfamiliarity with communicative and learner-centred approaches to learning and expectations of teacher and learner roles.

There may be linguistic factors which inhibit students such as:
- difficulties in transferring from the learner's first language to the sounds, rhythm and stress patterns of English
- difficulties with the native speaker pronunciation of the teacher
- a lack of understanding of common grammatical patterns in English (eg English tenses) and how these may be different from their own language
- lack of familiarity with the cultural or social language knowledge required to process meaning.

There may also be a range of psychological and affective factors including:
- culture shock, especially where newly arrived immigrants are coming to terms with the effects of resettlement in a new country
- previous negative social or political experiences, such as war or personal trauma
- lack of motivation, especially where they may not have chosen to learn, have negative views of the target language culture or do not see a purpose in learning the language
- anxiety and shyness in class, especially if previous learning and language learning experiences have been negative
- perceptions, some of which may also be cultural, (eg they are too old to learn a new language).

Reviewing factors that can affect language learning and attempting to identify the underlying reasons for students' reluctance to speak in class will help teachers to create the most positive environment for these learners. In some situations, and where facilities are available, it may be useful to involve educational counsellors and bilingual support. Talking to students one-to-one in a non-threatening situation may also be helpful.

Some theorists suggest that beginning learners may need a silent period during which they are given opportunities to listen, but are not required to produce the new language. Some learners who are reluctant to speak may benefit from classroom activities where they can respond physically or with only limited utterances.

The following strategies are suggested for students who are reluctant to speak in class:

- give students time to familiarise themselves with the classroom and with formal learning and acknowledge that a silent period of adjustment may be necessary
- introduce students to speaking activities through structured and guided practice that will provide them with success and increase their confidence
- provide opportunities to practise speaking through small group or pair work rather than requiring students to speak individually in front of the whole class
- give students tasks which involve concrete, familiar and short contributions rather than complex tasks with a number of simultaneous demands (eg speaking tasks that also require the student to read or write)
- provide structured support (eg personal response and drills) so that learners are reproducing familiar language already practised rather than new utterances
- create a structured and predictable classroom environment to increase confidence, and work on classroom dynamics so that students feel accepted and part of the group
- acknowledge progress on non-language outcomes such as bringing the correct equipment to class and organising folders of work as this may help to increase student confidence and motivation.

Further reading

Ellis, R. 1986. *Understanding second language acquisition*. Oxford: Oxford University Press.

Jackson, E. 1994. *Non-language outcomes in the language classroom: Curriculum guidelines*. Sydney: NCELTR and NSW AMES.

Lightbown, P. and N. Spada. 1993. *How languages are learned*. Oxford: Oxford University Press.

Larsen-Freeman, D. and Long, M. 1991. *An introduction to second language acquisition research*. New York: Longman.

10

How do I integrate speaking and listening?

In the past, listening – like reading – was sometimes considered to be a passive language skill. However, it is now generally recognised that listening is an interactive process which involves guessing, predicting, anticipating, organising, checking and interpreting. In situations where we are both speakers and listeners, listening becomes an active skill which plays an important part in shaping the talk. Rost (1990) for example suggests that listening is 'collaborative' with speaking as the listener must actively help the speaker to construct the interaction.

In relation to language learning, it is important to remember that learners are unlikely to be able to process language simply by hearing it; they must also be able to make sense of what they hear. They must be able to:

- segment the stream of sound and recognise word boundaries
- recognise stress patterns and rhythm
- recognise the vocabulary being used
- recognise grammatical patterns and structures
- attend to the meanings of what is being said
- create a coherent interpretation of these meanings
- activate appropriate social and cultural knowledge.

It is important, therefore, for language to be contextualised through teaching strategies such as concrete demonstrations, visual and text support, or through tasks that introduce learners to the sounds, vocabulary, grammatical patterns and cultural references involved in the interactions they will hear. Separate listening activities which provide learners with an opportunity to make predictions about contexts of language use or speaking tasks which occur within these context can be beneficial, especially at the beginning stages of learning. However, activities which treat listening as a macroskill to be taught in isolation do not always help learners to practise the listening skills that are needed outside the classroom. For example tasks such as asking learners to listen and then answer comprehension questions or to recall specific information after listening to a tape overlook the complementary and interactive nature of speaking and listening in spoken interactions.

More valuable is the provision of opportunities for integrated practice in speaking and listening. Strategies such as the following provide a basis for interactive speaking and listening activities in the classroom:

- encourage learners to use their social and cultural knowledge to predict the likely structure of the discourse in a particular context
- develop activities which require students to speak while they listen, rather than after they listen (eg taking different conversation roles related to specific contexts)

- provide listening tasks which place the student in the roles of the primary speakers and listeners (eg listening to a discussion about holiday plans and then telling another student about the places the speakers intend visiting)
- discuss with students the active relationship between listening which involves discourse strategies such as asking for clarification, indicating a comprehension problem, providing feedback to the speaker and so on
- provide activities where learners have to take alternate roles as listener and speaker (eg giving and receiving instructions for completing a task)
- discuss with learners taped or transcribed interactions where breakdown in communication seems to occur and analyse possible reasons and strategies
- discuss with learners some of the key features of spoken language (eg parataxis, ellipsis, turn taking and topic shifts) so that they can use this knowledge when listening and interpreting meanings.

Further reading

Anderson, A. and T. Lynch. 1988. *Listening*. Oxford: Oxford University Press.

Brewster, S. 1991. *Intermediate listening*. London: Nelson.

Rixon, S. 1986. *Developing listening skills*. London: Macmillan.

Rost, M. 1990. *Listening in language learning*. London: Longman.

Underwood, M. 1989. *Teaching listening*. London: Longman.